Assemblies for Infants

BOOK 2

Diane Walker

RMEP

RELIGIOUS AND MORAL EDUCATION PRESS

To Suzanne and Pamela and their dear families, and to Anthony, with my love.

Published by Religious and Moral Education Press
A division of SCM-Canterbury Press Ltd
A wholly owned subsidiary of Hymns Ancient & Modern Ltd
St Mary's Works, St Mary's Plain
Norwich, Norfolk NR3 3BH

First published 1999

ISBN 1 85175 171 8

Designed and typeset by Topics – The Creative Partnership, Exeter

Illustrations by Brian Platt

Printed in Great Britain by St Edmundsbury Press, Bury St Edmunds for SCM-Canterbury Press Ltd, Norwich

Contents

Contents (continued)

Introduction

Assemblies

The term 'assemblies' is used throughout this book for ease of reference. An 'assembly' is not necessarily the same as an 'act of worship', often applying to the 'school business' requirements of the meeting, rather than to its religious content. However, assembly remains the more widely used term.

Pupil integrity

Perhaps the most important factor to be taken into consideration when planning and delivering an assembly is that of pupil integrity. The position of each pupil must be respected, and agreement with views expressed or with religious statements made in the assembly should never be assumed. Statements of belief should always be introduced with distancing phrases, such as 'Christians believe...' and 'This is an important belief to Christians...'. This will respect and preserve the integrity of both teacher (presenter) and pupil. This practice is to be observed particularly at prayer-time. Pupils should not be compelled to join in with prayers, or to chorus the 'Amen' automatically, but should be given a choice. The prayer should be introduced with a phrase such as 'I am now going to say a Christian prayer. You may join in with the ''Amen'' at the end if you wish.' The prayers in this book are not preceded with such a phrase each time, and some invite pupil participation. But the fact that this is an invitation, and not an order, should be made abundantly clear to the pupils each time. At the same time, it should be made clear also that all of the pupils are expected to listen quietly and with respect: it is a two-way consideration. For the same reasons, the home situation of the pupils should always be borne in mind. Their participation in any part of the assembly which would compromise or oppose the ethos and beliefs expressed at home should be avoided. Similarly, any response from the pupils to the material which is itself respectful of different interpretations and is itself appropriately expressed should be accepted and valued.

Prayers and Reflections

Each assembly uses either a prayer or a reflection, or both. As stated above, the prayer should be introduced with a distancing phrase such as, 'Listen quietly while I read a Christian prayer. If you wish to, you can join in the ''Amen'' at the end.' Some of the prayers involve the pupils' participation, whether directly or indirectly. This should not be assumed or demanded. Reflections are intended to fulfil a different purpose. They invite the pupils to think privately about an issue. Pupils should not be expected to share these thoughts, although some may choose to do so later. It should be made clear to them that this is a private time. Often, a focal point is suggested, for both the prayers and the reflections. These are suggestions to encourage more focused attention from the pupils. Where no focal point is suggested, more general ones can be incorporated by the presenter, such as a lighted candle, a display, a view of the sky through a window. It is helpful to institute a recognized signal to mark the end of any thinking time. This could be a chord on the piano, a soft handclap or an agreed phrase, spoken quietly.

Preparation and planning

Many of these assemblies require only the minimum of preparation. Some do require more, but this is eased by the 'You will need' section at the beginning of the assembly. Every leader is called upon at some time to present an assembly with little or no warning. It is hoped that there are ample assemblies in this collection which would lend themselves to this 'one-off' requirement. At the same time, it is preferable that, wherever possible, each assembly fits into a prearranged plan, and that records are kept of assemblies presented. To this end, the assemblies are arranged in sections under named themes. Within each section, some assemblies do lead on from another assembly or assemblies, so enabling a development and reinforcement of a theme.

These are usually identified by the addition of a number to the title, e.g. Lent 1 and Lent 2. Some assemblies, of course, relate to the themes of more than one section. To facilitate easier cross-referencing, a thematic index has been included, and some links with other sections have been listed at the end of assemblies.

Contents of the sections

Most sections consist of the following parts:

You will need: this lists the items required during the presentation of the assembly.

Introduction: this is usually the part of the assembly which grounds the material in and relates it to the pupils' own experience. This is essential if the material is to have any relevance or meaning to them.

Core material: from the base of the Introduction, the next part of the assembly seeks to encourage the pupils to explore the theme in a wider Christian context. The core material presents the assembly's theme and explores its implications.

Prayer/Reflection: see above.

There are some exceptions to this basic plan, for instance the music assemblies.

Pupil participation

Pupil participation is built into the vast majority of the assemblies. It takes varying forms and degrees, ranging from the simple answering of questions, through singing, craft work and miming, to preparing and sharing their own work. Again, the pupils' integrity must be respected when selection is made. In some assemblies, the pupils participate in the prayers also.

Whole-class assemblies

There are some assemblies in this book to meet the needs of teachers who require an assembly in which their whole class can participate. Others can be adapted easily for this use.

Variety of content

The content of the assemblies is varied, and seeks to introduce a variety of stimuli to capture the pupils' interest and encourage their own consideration of the theme. These stimuli include stories of other countries, artefacts, nature and natural phenomena, other people, stories and history, everyday things, music and festivals. Some of the assemblies do deal with difficult concepts. A full understanding of these might be beyond some of the pupils at this stage, but the assemblies begin laying the groundwork to their understanding of these concepts in the future.

Atmosphere

A conducive atmosphere immediately before, during and after an assembly is vital if the pupils are to approach the assembly in a suitable frame of mind. Many schools have to use the assembly time to convey important information or news to the pupils. When this is the case, it is helpful to have a clear dividing line between the business part of the assembly and the 'worship' part. A change of presenter helps, or a statement that one part is over and the other beginning. A display or object which the pupils come to associate with assemblies – such as a table reserved for this use which could hold a focal point such as flowers or a candle – could be helpful in differentiating this use of the room from its other uses. Appropriate music for the pupils to enter and leave by helps to set this time apart from the normal business of the day and the room.

Music suggestions

There is a list of suggested songs related to the theme of each section. More general or familiar songs can, of course, be substituted.

Health and safety

Teachers are referred to their Health and Safety documents when any activity is suggested – especially during the Church Visit Assemblies, and when making objects.

Indexes

There are two indexes: one is a thematic index to simplify the search for an assembly on a particular theme, and the other is an index of the people, places, etc. mentioned in the assemblies. The contents page itself contains information about the content of each assembly.

Literacy

Much of the oral work and the activities in these assemblies complement the requirements of the Literacy Programme.

Acknowledgements

Many individuals have given generously of their time to provide me with the information I needed for this book. I am very grateful to all of them. Their names and organizations are listed below but I would like to add the names of Jan Walker, Sue Hatherly, Fleur and Sarah, Anna, Paul and Christopher, Kathleen and Yvonne, and Robin, my husband. Every effort has been made to trace information used. Any omissions are deeply regretted. Final responsibility for any error or omission lies with the author alone.

The information on page 29 (from *Fairground,* Primary Schools, Spring 1996) is used with the kind permission of CAFOD, Romero Close, Stockwell Road, London, SW9 9TY, and of Christian Aid (Banana Shake) address below.

The information on page 33 was supplied by the following organizations, and used with their kind permission: The Fairtrade Foundation, Suite 204, 16, Baldwin's Gardens, London, EC1N 7RJ; CAFOD (in *Fairground,* Primary Schools, Spring 1996) Romero Close, Stockwell Road, London, SW9 9TY, Christian Aid (in Banana Shake), address below.

The information on page 35 (from Global March against Child Labour and update from office) is used with the permission of Christian Aid, P.O. Box 100, London, SE1 7RT.

The material on page 37 is reproduced, with kind permission, from The Leprosy Mission's Magazine, *New Day,* No. 362. Further information can be obtained from The Leprosy Mission, Goldhay Way, Orton Goldhay, Peterborough, PE2 5GZ.

The information on page 39 (from The CAFOD Magazine, Summer 1998) is used with the kind permission of CAFOD, Romero Close, Stockwell Road, London, SW9 9TY.

The information on page 41 is used with the kind permission of A.I.M. (Africa Inland Mission), 2, Vorley Road, London N19 5HE.

The information on pages 49 (concerning the lighthouse) and 55 is used with the kind permission of Royal Sailors' Rests, 5, St. George's Business Centre, St. George's Square, Portsmouth, Hampshire, PO1 3EY: Tel. 01705, 296096; e-mail aggies@globalnet.co.uk; Website: www.rsr.org.uk.

The information on page 71 is used with the very kind permission of Southwell Minster, Southwell, Notts., and St. Mary's Church, Ottery St. Mary, Devon.

The banner on pages 76 and 117 is used with the kind permission of the Banner Making Group at St. Leonard's Church, Wollaton, Nottingham and of the artist, Veronica Boorman of Chilwell, Nottingham, and of the rector of the church, Canon David James.

The material on pages 97 and 99 is used with the kind permission of C.M.S., Partnership House, 157, Waterloo Road, London, SE1 8UU: it was used in the joint activity of A – Cross the World by C.M.S. and U.S.P.G. at Time Travelling! in Southwell Minster, 1998.

The words of the song 'We Are Marching in the Light of God' on page 102 are of African origin, collected and edited by Anders Nyberg. The music is an African melody scored by Notman KB, Ljungsbro and Lars Parkman. Arranged by R.T. Walker. The song is used with the kind permission of Iona Community/Wild Goose Publications, Glasgow, Scotland.

The music and text of the songs 'The Feeding of the Five Thousand', 'Light' and 'Jonah' on pages 103, 108 and 109 are used by kind permission of Sue Hatherly.

1 Mothering Sunday 1 – Simnel Cake

You will need

- a sheet of paper
- felt-tips

Introduction

Give the date of this year's Mothering Sunday, and ask if any of the pupils know what special day this is. Mothering Sunday is a day when we all have the chance to thank our mothers or anyone who looks after us for their hard work and love. Ask if any of the pupils are going to be buying or making presents for their mothers, and comment on these. Can they think of any other things that would make suitable presents? Years ago, many mothers would get the same presents – wild flowers and a cake!

About a hundred years ago, most girls and boys would have to work when they were not much older than the pupils. Many of the families in Britain were quite poor. Many children went away from home, to work in the big houses and on the big farms that belonged to richer people. They had to work very hard, and they hardly ever saw their parents. But once a year, they were allowed to go home on one Sunday, just to see their mothers and families. This Sunday was Mothering Sunday. The children would set off early, and walk to their homes, picking wild flowers on the way. (Point out that we are not allowed to pick wild flowers nowadays, because there are so few left.) The people who employed them often let them bake a cake to take with them. This would have cherries and nuts in it, and spices and butter. It was called a Simnel Cake. Many parts of England still have their old Simnel Cake recipe, and these cakes are still made.

This information about Mothering Sunday and the Simnel Cake is true. But there is a story about the first Simnel Cake – which may or may not be true! There was once a brother and a sister who were looking forward to going home to their mother on Mothering Sunday. The woman they worked for had told them they could make a cake for their mother, and they busily stirred and mixed the special ingredients she had given them. But when it was time to cook the cake, they couldn't decide how to do it. The boy said they should boil the cake – just as the cook boiled the sweet puddings he liked so much. But the girl said they should bake the cake in the oven, just as the cook baked the fruit cake at Christmas. They argued for a long time! In the end, they decided to do both – they boiled the cake and then they baked it as well! On Mothering Sunday, they proudly took the cake home, and their mother tried to cut it. It was very hard and very dry – and no one could eat it! The brother was called Simon and his sister was called Nell – and they decided to call the cake after both of them. So they took half of Simon's name and joined it onto some of Nell's name (demonstrate this with the felt-tips) – and the cake was called the Simnel Cake!

Nowadays, people still eat Simnel Cake, with cherries, spices, fruit and nuts in it – but people have decided that the best way to cook it is in the oven!

PRAYER

Thank you, Father, for all the hard work that our mothers and other carers do for us. Help us to remember to say thank you for this – all the year round, and not just on Mothering Sunday.

REFLECTION

Ask the pupils to look at their hands, and to think about something they could do today with those hands to show they care for someone.

LINK

Saying thank you, page 68

2 Mothering Sunday 2 – Our Simnel Cake

You will need

- two large circles of card – separate: one labelled 'Thank You for....', the other blank
- small pieces of paper – see below (these can be coloured/shaped to represent some of the traditional ingredients of Simnel Cakes – such as cherries, dried fruit, almonds, citrus peel, butter, eggs, etc.)
- felt-tips

Introduction

Remind the pupils about the Simnel Cake they heard about in the last assembly, and its use on Mothering Sunday. Ask them what other present children used to bring when they travelled home from their jobs. The cake and flowers were like thank you presents for their mothers. Explain that the pupils are going to make a thank you cake for their mothers/carers which they can display at school for them to see. Show them the two parts of the cake, reading out the words on the top. Just like a real cake, this cake needs ingredients, and the pupils are going to provide these. Show them the top layer of the cake once more. Does it look attractive? Do they think people seeing it will think it is good to look at? Talk about how cakes can be decorated.

One of the ways cakes are decorated is with flowers made out of icing. This would be a good way to decorate this cake, as the boys and girls used to take flowers as well as the Simnel Cakes to their homes. Invite some pupils to come out to decorate the top of the cake with flowers, making sure that the words can still be read clearly.

Can the pupils remember any of the ingredients from the Simnel Cake? If you have chosen to use colours and shapes for the ingredients, show the pupils the corresponding piece of paper as they name ingredients. If not, show them the small pieces of paper, and say that these are the ingredients of their cake. Each ingredient needs to be labelled with something for which they want to thank their mothers and carers. They can either write this or draw it. Start this off by labelling one – 'washing my clothes', for example – and then stick this onto the inside of the cake. Ask for other suggestions, inviting the pupils to come and write or draw what they say on one of the pieces of paper, and then to stick this onto the cake. Encourage the pupils to think about such things as love and listening, as well as the more practical things people do.

When this and the decoration are finished, stick the two layers together with a sellotape hinge at the top, so that the top can be lifted up to display the ingredients inside. This can then be hung in a common area of the school for parents and carers to look at.

REFLECTION

Hold the cake up so that the pupils can see the 'inside', and read through some of the 'ingredients' quickly. Ask them to choose one of these – or one of their own – for which they are grateful. Ask them to think about how they could show their mother or carer that they are grateful.

LINK

Saying thank you, page 68

3 Mothering Sunday 3 – Mother Church

Introduction

Many people have a special place – a place where they feel happy, or where they might feel safe when they feel unhappy. Share your special place with the pupils, or ask another (briefed) adult to share theirs. Invite the pupils to talk about their special place if they wish to, but make it plain that they do not have to do so. Alternatively, they may just wish to think about their own special place, and how it makes them feel, for a few moments. One special place for many people is their church. Christians believe that they can worship God and talk to him wherever they are. But they also believe that they need to meet together in a special place. There, they can learn about God, talk to him and to each other. Going to church is important for different reasons at different times for Christians. Several Christians of different ages were asked why church is a special place to them, and here are their answers. (Select from these according to time and appropriateness.)

Core material

'I go to church because I am a Christian. When I asked Jesus into my life and became his friend, I became part of God's family and God became my Heavenly Father. Church is a special place to me because it is in church that I meet with my brothers and sisters, God's family.' *Mother and grandmother*

'Church is a special place to me because I think church is God's house where he wants us to meet with more of his friends and to pray, sing songs of praise and treat each other like brothers and sisters. I also like learning more about God and his love for us all and being reminded how he would like me to live my life.' *Mother*

'Church is a special place to me because I go there to worship and learn about God. I like watching and listening to 'the spot' (in which people talk about God) and going to Pathfinders with other children of my own age at the end of the service.' *Twelve-year-old girl*

'Church is a special place to me. I go to church because I need God. His strength and guidance help me to cope with life's 'ups and downs'. God is with me all the time, but in church I feel closer to him – like visiting a friend. His power, strength and love are renewed within me.' *Yvonne*

'Church is a special place to me. I go to church because I get blessed ... .we do singing ... doing funny things, like when the vicar says something funny ... to learn about Jesus ... having a christening service ... we learn more about the world ... praying to God or Jesus ... to see what happens there. It's like being a big family and we belong there too. Seeing the parade service ... playing games in Explorers ... drawing round my feet in Climbers. ... To see if something exciting happens.' *Christopher, six, and Paul, ten*

'Church is a special place to me because it is somewhere I feel especially close to God. Sometimes it is very quiet but it is often noisy, but it is away from the normal daily rush.' *Teacher and father*

'Church is a special place to me because there I can meet and become friends with other Christians as well as growing as a Christian.' *Rebekah, seventeen*

'Church is a special place to me because it is a place where I can meet and talk to other Christians of my age. Also, it is a place where I can learn more about God.' *Rachael, fourteen*

Many people believe that Mothering Sunday started several hundred years ago because it was the day when people would go to their nearest big church. There, they would all meet together as one big family. The biggest church in each area of Britain was called the Mother Church. And that, some people believe, is where the name Mothering Sunday first came from.

REFLECTION

Some Christians said that one reason for going to church was that they enjoyed meeting with their friends, and talking to them. Ask the pupils to think about how they enjoy doing these things. To Christians, meeting with God is just like meeting with their friends.

Note

Book 1 in this series contains assemblies about the church, including one which deals with the Christian idea that the Church is God's people, not just the building in which they meet.

LINK

Church section, page 70

4 Lent 1 – Getting ready

You will need

- a large potato (or a lump of plasticine); make six holes in it beforehand – see below
- six feathers – real or paper
- globe or map
- an Advent calendar – used or unused

Introduction

Talk about the use of Advent calendars and, if appropriate, invite the pupils to tell you about the various kinds they had at Christmas. Discuss why some people have Advent calendars. They are to show how close a special time of the year is getting. As children open the doors, they grow more and more excited, because they can see that Christmas is coming at last. Some people use another sort of calendar like this. It isn't used to tell them when Christmas is coming, but another time of year which is special to them.

The six weeks leading up to Easter are called Lent. This doesn't mean that things are borrowed and lent during this time! It is a time when Christians all over the world think about their lives. Easter is near, and Christians believe that, at Easter, Jesus died so they could be friends with God. They believe their sins – the wrong things they have done – separate them from God. It is as if the wrong things are like a great valley. They believe they are on one side of the valley and God is on the other side. There is no bridge over the valley, and no other way to get across. Christians believe Jesus chose to die so he could be like the bridge over the valley. They believe that, because he died and rose again, they can cross the valley now and be friends with God. Christians believe God will forgive them for the wrong things they have done. But Christians do not believe this makes them perfect. They know they still do things wrong, because humans often choose to do the wrong thing instead of the right thing. It is easier to think about ourselves and to look after ourselves than to think about others and to do things to help them. So Christians believe they have to keep on asking God to forgive them. But they also believe God will help them to do the right things if they ask him to.

During Lent, Christians think especially about any wrong things they might have done. It is a time for looking at their lives, and checking they are living as God wants them to live. At the same time, they will ask God to help them to do the right things in the future. So Lent is a time for looking back and for looking forward. Christians believe they should do both these things before they celebrate Easter. Christians in Greece (show the pupils Greece on the globe or map) use a special sort of calendar to remind them that Lent is a special time. It is called a Kukaras, and it is made from a potato! (Show them the potato – or explain the substitute – and put the feathers in the holes as you speak.) There are six Sundays in Lent, and they put a feather in the potato for each Sunday. (Do this now.) Then, on each Sunday, they remove one feather. This reminds them of how close Easter is getting. Easter is a time of celebration and great happiness for Christians, because Jesus rose from the dead after the sadness of Good Friday when he died.

REFLECTION

It is good to have something special to look forward to! We often have to get things ready when something special is going to happen. Sometimes we have to get ourselves ready too! We have to dress in our best clothes, and make sure our hair looks right. For Christians, Lent is like getting themselves ready on the inside for a special time.

LINK

Easter section

5 Lent 2 – Getting rid of wrong things

You will need

- the potato or plasticine Kukaras, with the feathers in place
- six flags – made out of paper mounted on plastic drinking straws
- felt-tips

Introduction

Remind the pupils of the theme of the last assembly: during Lent, Christians look back at the things they have done wrong and say sorry for them, and look forward to the future, when God will help them not to do those things again. Remind them of the use of the Kukaras and ask what the feathers represent. Explain that together you are going to replace the feathers with flags, and show them the flags. The real Kukaras lasts for six weeks, of course, but you are going to use it just for today. It can then stay on view to remind everyone what they talked about during the assembly.

Christians think about the things they have done wrong. One of these things could be being selfish. Discuss what this means, perhaps asking for (hypothetical) examples. Then write it on one of the flags, and ask a pupil to remove a feather from the Kukaras and replace it with the flag. Ask the pupils if they can think of other things Christians might have to say sorry for during Lent. Repeat the exercise until all the flags are in place. (Make it clear that you are not asking what they or anyone else have actually done wrong.)

These are some of the things that Christians might have done wrong. They will say sorry for them – but that is only half the message of Lent. Christians also try, with God's help, not to do those things again. Name each wrong thing, and ask the pupils what the opposite of each of them would be. (Sometimes they will not be able to produce an exact opposite. Encourage them to think of behaviour that would have the opposite effect to the wrong thing, e.g. if they said stealing, they could now think about looking after other people's property.) As each 'opposite' is named, remove the relevant flag, and write it on the back in a different colour. These are the things that Christians will try to do during the next year. Replace the flags.

PRAYER

Thank you, Father, that you are ready to forgive people when they have done wrong things. Thank you that you help your followers not to do those things again. Thank you that, even if they do, you are still ready to forgive them and to help them try again.

LINK

Easter section, page 80

6 Candlemas

You will need

- candles – to be lit if there is a safe place

Tell this old story from Germany. All through the cold winter, the badger slept deep underground in his den (sett), warm and snug in his bed of dry grass. Now it was time to wake up – February 2nd. He yawned and stretched, and then crept along the tunnel that led to the outside world. He looked outside at the weather. It was warm and fine. 'Oh dear!' he thought – and turned round and went back to bed! Soon, he was fast asleep again. But if the weather had been wet and cold, he would have left his warm tunnels, and gone outside to find food.

LINK

Light section

What a strange badger! He went back to bed because the weather was fine and warm! He would have got up if it was cold and wet! What sort of weather would the pupils expect the badger to like? Of course, this is only a story. The badger does not really always wake up on the same day each year. He doesn't really go back to bed if the weather is good then, or get up if it is bad. But this story was made up years ago because people believed they could tell what the weather was going to be like for the whole of the Spring by looking at the weather on February 2nd. They believed that, if the weather was good on that day, the rest of the Spring would be very cold and wet. But if the weather was bad on that day, then Winter was really over and the good weather was just about to begin. So a story was made up in which the badger knew what the weather was going to be like as well.

The badger isn't the only animal who is supposed to know this. In America, a similar story is told about the groundhog (woodchuck). Again, the groundhog goes back to sleep if the weather is good, but gets up if the weather is bad! Discuss what the weather is telling us or told us on this day this year!

Of course, this is just a story, and we can't rely on it being true! But February 2nd is a special day to many people for other reasons. It even has a special name – Candlemas Day. Here, 'mass' means a festival or special day. What do the pupils think the first part of the name refers to? Candle-mas was the day when the candles which would be used in church during the next year were brought into the church. Ask the pupils why candles were so important to people in the past that they had a special day for them. Talk about how they would light the church, and what a difference the candles would make on a dark winter's day. Some churches are very dark even in the middle of a summer's day! For Christians, candles are important for another reason, too. They remind them of Jesus. He said he was the Light of the World. (If the assembly on this has already been used, remind the pupils of what he meant. If not, use this brief account: Christians believe Jesus meant several things when he said this. He could show people the way to be friends with God, just as a light can guide people in the darkness. He also meant people could feel safe with him as their friend, just as a light helps us to feel safe on a dark night.) So the people were very glad to store enough candles for the whole year safely in church, and they spent time thanking God for them.

REFLECTION

Light the candles and ask the pupils to imagine what their homes would be like in the long winter evenings with just candles to light them and no electricity. Then ask them to imagine how pleased they would be with the light from candles if that was the only light they had! Add the prayer if appropriate.

PRAYER

Thank you, Father, that it is so easy for us to light our homes and other buildings.

7 Abraham – Trusting God

You will need

- three stickers, suitable for sticking on pupils' clothes
- a timer or egg-timer (one minute)

Introduction

Choose three pupils to come out. (Choose the third one with care, bearing in mind the demands about to be made on them!) Say you are going to give them each a sticker – but not at the same time. Give one pupil a sticker immediately. Tell the next s/he has to wait until the timer goes off. Set it for a minute, first asking everyone to wait in silence until the time is up. At the end of the time, give the second pupil the sticker. Then tell the last one that you promise you will give them the sticker – but they have to wait until you are ready. Ask this pupil to sit at the front until then. Stress that you do promise you will give it to them.

Ask the first pupil if it was easy waiting for their sticker. Then ask the second one. Even one minute can seem long. There is a story in the Bible about a man who had to wait a very long time for something God had promised to give him. The man was called Abraham. (Tell the story below, pausing at points of your own choosing to reassure the third pupil you will give them the sticker. Congratulate them – if appropriate! – on their patience.)

Abraham lived in a very comfortable house in a rich city with his wife Sarah. They were rich themselves, and owned many servants and animals. One day, God said to Abraham, 'I want you to leave your home. Take Sarah and your animals and travel to a new land which I will give you and your children to live in.' So Sarah and Abraham got ready to leave. It was difficult to know what to take with them, because God hadn't told them what sort of country it was. Would it be hot and dry? Or would it be cold and wet? They packed up big leather tents to live in on their journey. They hoped they would soon be able to build themselves proper houses!

Abraham and Sarah set off. They thought they would soon arrive in their new country and be able to settle down, but when they arrived, they did not find any land which they could take as their own. They had to ask other people if they could camp on their land! They couldn't settle down in one place, because they had to keep travelling on to find new water and grass for their animals. The tents became old and battered from being taken down and put up so many times, and the wind kept blowing holes in them. God kept telling them this was the land he would give to them – but they still didn't own any of it. God also told them there would be hundreds of people in their family in the future – but Abraham and Sarah still didn't have even one child! In fact, Sarah was now too old to have children! But they always remembered God's promises. He had promised them a land of their own and a big family. At last, many years after they had left their own city, they had a son of their own, and they were able to settle in their new land. Abraham was sure that, in the future, his family would be very big and that they would own all the land in this new country, just as God had promised him so many years before. It was not easy for Abraham to keep on trusting God and believing he would keep his promises. Ask the third pupil if they are getting impatient yet. It is hard to wait for someone to keep their promise.

Just before the pupils are dismissed, give the sticker to the third pupil, thanking them for their patience.

REFLECTION

God kept his promise to Abraham and Sarah. Can other people rely on you to keep your promises?

LINK

Trust – 'The Man who Came Through the Roof', page 60; 'The Girl', page 64; 'The Man who said Thank you', page 68

8 Samuel – Listening to God

You will need

- simple notices/information for various pupils or teachers in school – see Introduction

Introduction

Arrange to have several simple messages or notices for people in school available, and ask some pupils to deliver these orally for you to the relevant people. Ensure the other pupils hear who each message is for, and check with them each time that the message was accurate and that it was taken to the right person. Comment at the end that it could be disastrous if a message is taken to the wrong person. It wouldn't matter if the message was accurate if the wrong person received it. (You could illustrate this if you wish by asking what would have happened if a particular message of yours had gone to someone else instead.) A messenger has to make sure they have the message right and that they take it to the right person.

Core material

When Samuel was still a young boy, he found out he was going to be God's messenger, taking God's messages to people. (If the pupils have heard the assembly on page 47 of Book 1 in this series or already know the story, ask them if they can tell you what happened when Samuel was a boy with Eli in the Temple. If not, tell the story briefly, as follows.) Samuel lived in the Temple, which was where people came to worship God. He helped Eli the priest. Eli was old. When Samuel heard someone calling him in the middle of the night, he thought it was Eli asking him to help him. But Eli told him it was God calling him. God gave Samuel a message for Eli. This was the first of many messages that God gave Samuel to give to other people. Samuel always listened carefully, making sure that he got the message right and that he took it to the right person. But one day, when Samuel was an old man himself, God gave him a message to take to someone – and Samuel wasn't sure who it was!

'It is time to choose the next king,' God told Samuel. The king was Saul, but Saul had not obeyed God. God sent Samuel to anoint the man who would be Israel's next king. This meant he was to pour special oil on the man's head as a sign that he was to be king. Samuel listened to God. He found out where he should go, and set off for the small town of Bethlehem. There, he went to the house of a man called Jesse. 'I want to see your sons,' he told Jesse. Up to now, Samuel had got the message right. He knew the next king would be one of Jesse's sons. The trouble was – he did not know which one it would be. 'Never mind!' he thought. 'When I see them, I will know which one it should be. Our next king should be a grown-up man, strong and tall.' Samuel watched as the sons came out to meet him. As soon as he saw the eldest son, he thought, 'Yes! It must be him!'

He got ready to anoint him – and God said, 'No! That's not the right man!' So Samuel watched the next son. He was tall and handsome as well, and he looked as if he was very clever. But God said again, 'No! That's not the man!' This carried on until seven sons had gone by. Samuel was puzzled. 'Haven't you any more sons?' he asked Jesse. Jesse told him he did have one more son called David, but he was only a young boy. He was looking after the sheep in the hills. Samuel asked Jesse to send for David, and soon he came, wondering what the matter was. As soon as Samuel saw the boy, God said, 'This is the king!' So Samuel anointed David, and then David went back to look after the sheep. Samuel realized that God knew much more about people than he did. He knew that David was just the person he wanted to be king, even though his big brothers had looked as if they were right for the job! All Samuel had to do was listen to God.

PRAYER

Thank you, God, that you can choose just the right person for each job. Thank you that you know everything about us, and still love us.

REFLECTION

Ask the pupils to think about whether they are good listeners or not.

LINK

Church Visit Assemblies, 'Kneelers', page 78

9 Daniel – Standing up for God (a whole-class assembly)

You will need

- a class of pupils – one run-through would help them learn their speeches and follow your text; words in italics are instructions; choose Daniel with care
- a rolled-up piece of paper as a scroll

Introduction

Start off with one pupil, A, at one side of the 'stage', the rest at the other. Sometimes, it is easy to stand up for what we believe is right. *Another pupil, B, crosses to A and says, 'Don't do any work today!' A replies, 'No, I'm going to work!'* Sometimes, it is harder to stand up for what you believe in. *The action is repeated, with four more pupils joining B. A still refuses.* Sometimes, it is very, very difficult to stand up for what you believe in! *The class shouts, 'We're not doing any work today!' A takes one step towards them, then back, and repeats this: s/he does not know what to do.* It is easy to stand up for what you believe is right when only one person disagrees with you. But it is not easy when many people disagree with you.

There is a story in the Bible about a man who stood up for what he believed was right, even though many people were against him, and even though he knew these people were very powerful and could have him killed! His name was Daniel. *Stand a pupil as Daniel at one side of the 'stage', one as King Darius at the other side, and the rest of the pupils as Daniel's enemies in the middle, telling the pupils who everyone is. The pupils can mime the action as you read. Give the scroll to one of the crowd: they can pretend to read the King's orders as you read them. Pause where necessary throughout the story to allow the pupils time to perform their actions.*

This is Daniel *(point to him).* Daniel did not live in his own country. He had been taken to Babylon when the King of Babylon had defeated David's country. There, he worked for the king. The King at that time was Darius. *Point to Darius.* He was very vain and thought he was the best king ever. Daniel worked hard, and Darius gave him an important job. The other people who worked for the King *(point to them)* were jealous and angry *(they shake their fists at Daniel).* They decided to get rid of Daniel. They told the King that he was so important people should ask only him for help and no one else. So Darius made it a new law and a messenger read it out: 'No one can pray to anyone except the King. If they do, they will be thrown to the lions!' *(A pupil 'reads' from the scroll.)*

Daniel listened to the law. Then he went home. He went to the window of his room, knelt down, lifted his arms, and prayed to God, just as he did every day. He did not worship the gods of Babylon. He still worshipped God, and God had said that his people must not worship anyone else but him. Daniel's enemies watched him. They had trapped him. They hurried to the King. They were very happy, but the King was miserable. That night, he had to throw Daniel into the pit where the lions were kept. All night, Darius walked round and round his room. He could not sleep, he was so worried. In the morning, he rushed to the pit, shouting Daniel's name. And Daniel said, 'I am all right, Darius! God has looked after me. The lions did not touch me!'

So God kept Daniel safe. Darius made a new law: 'Everyone should know that Daniel's God is very powerful and that he looks after his people.'

REFLECTION

Daniel did not know for sure that God would keep him safe. But he knew that he could not worship anyone but God. He knew he had to obey God. He knew that God loved him. He was willing to risk his life to show that he loved God. Ask the pupils to think about whether they do the right thing only when it is easy and safe.

LINK

'People as Lights', pages 50 and 52; 'Kneelers', page 78

10 Jonah – Disobeying God

Note

This assembly is to be followed by the music assembly 'Jonah' on page 110.

You will need

- some messages – see Introduction and page 22

Introduction

[Repeat the message delivery on page 22, but this time brief one pupil to refuse to deliver a message to one of the adults present, whatever you say to them. They could walk over to the other side of the hall and stay there. When you ask them why they won't deliver the message, they are to say that they don't want to.] A messenger is not much good if they decide whether or not to deliver the message! The people who deliver our post each day are like messengers, because they are bringing other people's messages to us. Ask the pupils what would happen if a postman said, 'I'm not taking that parcel anywhere! It's too heavy!' Or if a postwoman said, 'I'm not delivering any letters to the people in those new houses. I don't like them!'

Jonah was one of God's messengers. God told him what to say and who he was to tell it to. Jonah was happy to do this for a while. He took God's messages to the Israelites, and they listened to him. But one day, God gave him a message for some other people – and Jonah refused to go.

'Go to the city of Nineveh,' God said. 'Tell them I have seen how badly they behave, and how they hurt other people. I will not let this carry on. Tell them I will destroy their city.'

Jonah shook his head. 'I'm not going there!' he said. 'You know how cruel they are! They might kill me!' And he set off to walk in the opposite direction – to the sea! 'If I go to Nineveh, I know what will happen,' he thought. 'They will say sorry for doing wrong things, and God is so loving that he will forgive them. They have done wrong, and they should be punished for it. I don't want God to forgive them, so I will not give them his message!'

He paid the captain of a ship to take him away from Nineveh, but as soon as they set sail, a terrible storm blew up. Jonah realized that God had sent the storm to stop him, and he told the sailors to throw him into the sea, so they would be safe. As soon as he was in the sea, the storm stopped. Jonah sank down and down – but then God sent a huge fish which swallowed him. For three days and nights, Jonah was in the dark insides of the fish. In the end, he told God he was sorry for disobeying him. God made the fish spit Jonah out onto the shore, and Jonah walked into Nineveh.

As soon as he told the people there what God had said, they said sorry to God. And God said he forgave them. Jonah was furious. He stamped out of the city, and went to sit on a hill to sulk. There, God sent a plant to shade him from the sun. But next day, God sent a worm which hungrily ate through the plant's stem, so the plant died. Jonah was sorry to see the plant die, because it had shaded him from the sun. God said to him, 'Are you really sorry just because this plant has died?' and Jonah told him that he was. God went on, 'You didn't even make the plant, but its death has made you sad. There are hundreds of people living in Nineveh. Why shouldn't I want them to live long and happy lives instead of being destroyed?'

Jonah could not think of anything to say after this. He realized that God loved the people of Nineveh as well as the Israelites, and he was sorry he had disobeyed him.

PRAYER

Thank you, Father, that you love all people everywhere, and that you want to forgive all of them for the wrong things they have done.

REFLECTION

Christians believe Jonah had to learn that God's love and forgiveness is for all people. They believe that God wants other people to hear this, just as he wanted the people of Nineveh to hear about his love.

LINK

'Jonah', page 110; ***Saying sorry*** and ***Forgiveness,*** pages 14, 16, 26, 90

11 Chocolate Bananas

You will need

- a bunch of bananas
- bars of chocolate, including cooking chocolate
- prepared 'chocolate banana' (banana peeled and halved lengthwise, with melted chocolate poured over it; if the chocolate could be melted immediately before the assembly, this could be prepared in front of the pupils)
- cocoa beans (if possible; if not, coffee beans)
- pen and paper for teacher's use

Introduction

Ask how many pupils like bananas and how many like chocolate. How many like the two together? Show the prepared dessert, or prepare it now – see above. Show the 'raw' materials, including the cooking chocolate. Ask them to give you accurate instructions for making this dessert, making sure they do things in the right order. In this and the next two assemblies, we are going to look at the two ingredients of this dessert: chocolate and bananas. Ask the pupils to tell you anything they know about these two foods, and then adapt the following information to take account of what they have said.

Bananas grow on trees in warm countries, such as the islands in the Caribbean. They grow in bunches – ask the pupils which way up they think they grow, and then demonstrate with the bunch, holding them so they grow upwards. Discuss how they are brought to this country in very big ships. Ask the pupils the colour of most of the bananas we eat. They grow in other colours too, such as green and pink! Yellow bananas are green when they are unripe. Ask what happens if a banana becomes too ripe. If we want to eat them when they are just right – yellow and firm – bananas have to be packed when they are still unripe. Explain that the people who bring them to this country know how to stop the bananas getting too ripe while they are travelling. The people who grow the bananas have to know just the right time to pick them, and the packers have to pack them very carefully so they are not damaged.

Ask the pupils how we use bananas in this country. Some of them may have eaten dried banana slices. In the countries where they grow, bananas and the banana trees are used in many different ways. Here are some: bananas can be sliced up and fried like chips, and eaten for breakfast with egg and bacon; they can be made into flour to make cakes; the leaves can be used as thatch on house roofs, or used as umbrellas when it rains; the leaves can be used as shopping baskets and to make lampshades. Pupils could mime these uses if you wish.

What about chocolate? Ask if any of the pupils know what is in chocolate. One of the main ingredients is cocoa. Do any of them know how cocoa grows? Show the beans if you were able to get any. If you have coffee beans, explain that cocoa beans are quite like these. Discuss what people would have to do to these hard beans before they could make chocolate from them. How do we use it in this country? Ask the pupils to name their favourite 'uses' of chocolate. In one of the countries where cocoa grows, people used to use the beans as money! We'll find out how tomorrow!

PRAYER

Discuss with the pupils how some foods go well together – like fish and chips! Invite them to suggest other foods which they like to eat together. Make a note of these, and incorporate them in the prayer:

Thank you, God, for the many different foods we can enjoy in this country. Thank you that some of them taste so nice together – like chocolate and bananas, … .

REFLECTION

We can't grow bananas in this country because of the climate. Help the pupils to think of other foods they enjoy which we cannot grow here. Then ask them to imagine never being able to eat these foods from other countries again. Perhaps they could ask their families tonight what they would miss.

12 Chocolate Money

You will need

- chocolate coins
- enlarged copy of Fairtrade logo – off wrapper of following item
- a bar of Maya Gold chocolate
- cocoa beans (if possible; if not, coffee beans)
- real 5p and 10p coins
- a table set up as a shop with a few items priced at 5p and 10p

Introduction

Ask an adult to act as the shopkeeper. Ask two pupils to buy one or more items from the shop, depending on age, and to select the coins they need to buy these. Then ask two more pupils to buy set items, but give them the chocolate coins. The shopkeeper should refuse to sell the items. Ask the two pupils why the shopkeeper would not take their money. Ask them to show the money to the other pupils, and to explain to them what it is made of. Many children are given this money – at Christmas especially. These coins are good to eat, but it would not be much good trying to use them to buy something in a shop! But once, it was a different story.

Recap on what was said in the last assembly about cocoa beans being used as money. Years ago, around 600 AD, there were some people living in South America whom we call the Maya Indians. They lived in great stone cities. They discovered cocoa beans growing in the jungles around their homes. They made a drink out of these – but it was very different from our own hot chocolate drink! Ours is a sweet drink: theirs was hot and spicy. (Some pupils may have tasted a similar drink at Cadbury World, in Bournville, Birmingham.) It was very popular, and soon cocoa beans were so important and valuable that the Maya Indians began to use them as money to buy other things they needed!

The Maya Indians became rich because of cocoa beans. But it is very different for their descendants today. Now, the people who grow and harvest cocoa beans are very poor. They are not paid a fair price for the beans or for their work. Several organizations and companies are trying to change this. One company is the maker of this chocolate bar (show them the Maya Gold chocolate bar). Notice the name: they have named it after the Maya Indians. The wrapper has a symbol on it (show the symbol on the bar and in its enlarged form). This means that this chocolate is produced by a firm that pays a fair wage to its workers, and makes sure that they have good houses and living conditions. So at last the cocoa beans that were valuable, like gold, to the Mayan Indians are becoming valuable again to the people who grow them today.

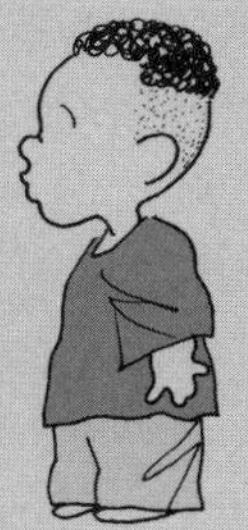

PRAYER

Thank you, Father, for the different flavours of the foods you have given to us. As we enjoy them, help us to remember the people who work hard to bring the food to us, and to do all we can to make their lives easier when they are in need.

REFLECTION

Close your eyes for a few minutes and listen. Imagine you are eating your favourite chocolate bar. Chocolate does not cost much in this country, but it is still a luxury – something we don't really need. But some of the people who grow and harvest the cocoa beans cannot even afford the things they really need. Next time you enjoy chocolate, remember these people. Perhaps you could try one of the bars like the Maya bar; buying them helps these people.

LINK

Working for others, pages 10, 32, 34, 36, 38, 40, 50, 52, 54, 60, 94

13 Fair-share Bananas

You will need

- a large picture of a banana, plus enlarged sections, showing amounts, to fit onto it (see page 114)
- notices for pupils to hold up: the person who grows the banana; the person who packs it; the person who owns the ship; the people who buy the banana and bring it into Britain; the people who sell the banana to the shopkeeper; the shopkeeper who sells you the banana (this list can be simplified as necessary, and pictures used instead of words)
- Blutak

Introduction

Remind the pupils of the dessert. We have thought about chocolate. Ask them what the other ingredient was. Bananas grow a very long way away from our country. A lot of people take part in a banana's journey to our homes. Go through the following, asking the pupils what they know about each one and supplying the missing information. As each job is discussed, ask two pupils to come out and hold the relevant notice so the others can see it. Make sure they stay in the right order.

Core material

1 ***The growers.*** **Growing bananas is hard work. The land has to be cleared, and other plants and trees cut down. The soil has to be carefully dug. It takes nine months for the bananas to grow from the flower to a banana ready to pick. All that time, the grower has to look after the bananas. He has to work every day. If there is a strong wind, all of the bananas might be blown off the trees. The trees themselves might be blown down! Every year, the grower has to spend half the money he earns on new plants and sprays for the next year. So if he earned one pound, how much would he have left? The grower would still have food and clothes to buy for his family.**

2 *The packers.* The packers have to pack the fruit very carefully so that they don't damage it.

3 *The ship owner.* The ship owner has to know how to keep the bananas just right so that they don't become too ripe. He takes the fruit to Britain.

4 *The importer* (explain what this means). Usually, it is large (multinational) companies which buy the fruit off the grower and pay for it to come to Britain.

5 *The wholesaler* (explain what this means). He stores a lot of fruit in big buildings, and the shopkeepers buy the fruit they want in their shops from the wholesaler.

6 *The shopkeeper.* The shopkeeper buys the fruit and displays it on the shelves for you to buy.

Ask the pupils to think for a few minutes about which job they think is the most important and which is the hardest. Which person do they think should get the most money? Discuss their answers as time allows, and try to reach a decision on who should get the most. Then display the big banana. We will say a banana costs 20p. Who did they decide should get most of this money? Ask pupils to hold up the banana while you stick on the amounts in the correct places. Then comment on the results, and the actual distribution of money. Do the pupils think the money is shared out fairly? Why/why not? When people are given a fair share of the money their own fruit earns, it is called fair trading. (For younger pupils, the workers can be simplified into two groups – growers and the others.)

There are many people who are working to make the sharing of this money fairer. It was easy to see which chocolate had been fairly traded because of the Fairtrade Mark. It is not easy to see which bananas have been fairly traded. Some people are now trying to get the Fairtrade Mark on bananas which have come from growers who are treated fairly.

Note

No pupil should be left with a feeling of guilt because of inequalities they are not in a position to remedy in any way. The aim should be simply to raise their awareness of such issues.

PRAYER

Thank you that we can enjoy foods from many countries. As we grow up, help us to remember the people who work hard to provide us with our food.

REFLECTION

We might not be able to help the people who grow fruit many miles away, but we can make sure we treat other people fairly here. Ask the pupils to think whether they are treating people fairly in school and at home.

LINK

Working for others, pages 10, 30, 34, 36, 38, 40, 50, 52, 54, 60, 94

14 School – and Work

You will need

- several nets of two parts of matchbox (see page 114) cut out in stiff card – suitable for folding by pupils – with folds scored
- a matchbox with matches
- a globe or world map
- paper, felt-tips, scissors
- glue or sticky tape

Introduction

Ask for volunteers to help you make something. Give each one a net, and ask them if they can work out what it is. Show them how to fold each shape, and glue or tape it, and then pair them up. Show how this makes a matchbox like those used by people in Britain. Ask the volunteers how many matchboxes they think they could make in a day. If they spent all day on the work, do they think they could make a thousand of them? Could they make a thousand if they had to come to school every day as well?

Core material

Jeylakshmi lives in South India (show the pupils where this is). She loves going to school and learning new things. She gets up very early and is ready to work by seven o'clock. She works for two hours until it is time for school. Then, at break, she rushes home to work again. After school, she works until seven o'clock. For Jeylakshmi has to make matchboxes every day just so that her family can have enough to eat and clothes to wear. She can make a thousand boxes a day, as well as going to school. She doesn't have much time for playing! Her father works all day, too, making and selling poppadoms (explain). But he can only earn about 2p a day. So Jeylakshmi has to work.

Jeylakshmi is only one of many thousands of children in different countries around the world who have to work. Many of them cannot even go to school because they have to work all day. Others, like Jeylakshmi, go to school, but don't have time for any of the things we take for granted, such as playing with friends. When children have to work like this it is called child labour. Christian Aid is one of many organizations which are trying to change this. They want the governments of all countries to get rid of child labour. Ask for suggestions about how this could be done. Stress that it is no good just stopping the child labour: the families need the money for essentials, not for luxuries. One way, for instance, is to increase the wages of the adults in a family in some way. But this, of course, is not easy in some countries.

In 1998, Christian Aid organized a 'Global March'. Discuss why it was called this. People joined together to march from Asia, Africa, Latin America and Europe to Geneva in Switzerland. Show the pupils where these places are on the map. In Geneva, they spoke to the United Nations – explain that this is a group of countries that work together to give people help when they need it. Of course, not everyone who wanted to get rid of child labour could go on this march. So instead, they drew round their feet, and then sent their footprints to Christian Aid, to show how many people disagree with child labour. All of the footprints were handed in at 10, Downing Street (talk about significance of this) and some were sent on to Geneva for the meeting held there about child labour. Some of the footprints were sent to a centre in India where children who used to have to work are now being helped. So these children know that other children, miles away from India, knew about them and were trying to help. Many children have already been helped, and people are still working hard to help the others who have to work.

REFLECTION

PRAYER

Ask your volunteer workers to draw round one foot each and cut it out. Ask all the pupils to tell you what they would like to happen to help child workers throughout the world. Either write these wishes on the feet, or ask the pupils to turn them into prayers and write these on the feet. The sentences can be read out as either a Reflection or a Prayer, and the feet can be displayed in the assembly area.

LINK

Working for others, pages 10, 32, 36, 38, 40, 50, 52, 54, 60, 94

15 The Lamplighters

You will need

- (if possible) pictures of gas street lamps and/or a lamplighter
- if completed, the poster on sources of light (see page 42)
- a sheet of paper and pens

Introduction

(Use the poster for the introductory activity, or ask for sources of light and describe each as necessary for the pupils.) People have used many ways of making light through the years! But how did they 'switch on' each method? Go through sources of light, on the poster or orally, asking pupils to mime how each is 'switched on'. Ensure gas lamps are included, describing how these were lit and controlled. Talk about the tall gas street lamps, once used to light streets, and about the lamplighter who used to come round each evening to light the lamps, using a flame on a long pole , and return each morning to put out the flames. When the lamplighter came, people could tell roughly what time it was – just as we might say, 'Come on, time to get up – the paper's arrived!'

In 1947, a lot of children became Lamplighters – but they didn't light any gas lamps! They were a different sort of lamplighter – one that is mentioned in the Bible! They joined a club or organization, like Boys' and Girls' Brigades, fan-clubs, or Rainbows and Beavers. They wore badges with lamps on them, and they made a promise when they joined, which we'll hear later on.

Note
The asterisked text is used in the assembly on page 68.

Core material

***Leprosy is a disease. There are stories in the Bible about people with leprosy. (If appropriate, refer to the story on page 68.) Today, at least five million people suffer from leprosy. We know a lot more about leprosy now than they did in**

Bible times. We know it does not spread very easily from one person to another. Many people cannot catch it. But years ago people thought it was very easy to catch leprosy. They made people with leprosy leave their families and homes and live by themselves, with no one to look after them.* This still happens in some countries, but many people are working hard to change this. The Leprosy Mission is a group of people who know a lot about leprosy. They work in many countries, looking after people with leprosy. They give them the medicines they need to stop the disease getting worse. The biggest problem that leprosy causes is that it takes away the feeling in people's skin. Ask the pupils what they would do if they trod on something sharp. People with leprosy can't always feel pain like this, so they don't stop doing the thing that is damaging their bodies. They can injure themselves very badly. The people who work for The Leprosy Mission help prevent this happening. They help people who have leprosy find new jobs which won't hurt them, so they can look after their families again.

In 1947 The Leprosy Mission decided to start clubs called Lamplighters. In these clubs, the children met together to play games, and to learn about the work of the Mission. They collected money to send to the people working to help people with leprosy. For many years, these clubs raised a lot of money. Today, only one club is still going! It is still called the Lamplighters, and it meets at St. John's Church, at Welling. It is such a popular club that there is a waiting list to join it! They still collect money to send to the people who work for the Mission, and they write to one of its workers.

People don't have to be members of the Lamplighters to help The Leprosy Mission! Many other people, including children, help the Mission. When Lamplighters join, they promise to 'light the lamp of love for people with leprosy.' Jesus said people should be like lights or lamps for others. He meant that people should try to make life easier for others in whatever way they can. Anyone can be this sort of 'lamplighter', just by the way they behave each day, as they go to school or work, go shopping or talk to their neighbours.

REFLECTION

PRAYER

Draw a large lamp in the middle of the sheet of paper, and rays of light streaming out from it. Ask the pupils to suggest people who are working to help others who need help, such as doctors and nurses. Write their suggestions in the beams of light. Then either ask the pupils to think about these people and how they help others, or make up a prayer thanking God for them, which could begin:

Thank you, God, for the many doctors and scientists who have found out more about diseases through the years, so that ill people can be looked after. Thank you for the people who are working here and in other countries today to help others.

LINK

'People as Lights', pages 50 and 52; 'Light', page 42; 'The Man who Said Thank You', page 68

16 Dipping and Making Candles

Note

This assembly can use pre-dipped candles. It would be interesting, however, for pupils to see the process of dipping, although time precludes including the entire procedure in one assembly. Dipping ready-made white candles allows them to understand the process. Instructions for dipping are given on page 115. Perhaps the candles could be burned during subsequent assemblies, especially during Reflections.

(**NB** If dipping is done during the assembly, precautions are needed to make it safe. It would not be advisable to involve pupils in the actual dipping. They can decide which colours are used on each candle, and in which order.)

You will need

- a large bucket of cold water, easily accessible at all times
- plain white household candles
- two pots of coloured wax, pre-melted (see page 115)
- metal tongs for lowering the candles into the wax
- old cloths (e.g. tea-towels) and heatproof gloves
- wick
- unmelted wax (see page 115)

Introduction

Tell the pupils you are dipping candles today. Explain you are going to be using a very hot liquid and must be very careful. Show them the water, and say it is there in case you splash any wax on your hands accidentally. That would hurt! Explain that, if you had time, you would make the candles from just wax and wick – show them the pieces of wax and wick. Show or tell them what happens to the wax when it is heated. Describe how the wick can be dipped into the hot wax again and again. Each time, more wax sticks to the wick, and it grows fatter and fatter, until it is thick enough to be used as a candle. Today, you do not have time for this, so you are going to cheat! Show them a ready-made candle. Dip it into one of the pots and then in the water, and then hold it up to show them the result. Repeat the process with the other colour. Invite the pupils to choose the colour/s of other candles, and then dip them as asked.

Core material

How might these candles be used? When do we use candles nowadays? At one time in this country they were the only source of light in many homes. In many countries today, this is still true. In one of the villages in the Maphumulo district of KwaZulu province in South Africa, the children find it very difficult to do their homework. They can't read their books in the evenings, either. If one of them is ill in the night, it is very difficult for their parents to look after them. It can be dangerous to walk along the paths of the village at night. This is because they have no electricity in their village at all! Ask the pupils to think for a few minutes about all the things they themselves could not do if they had no electricity. Ask how they think the children manage at night and in the evening. For them, candles aren't just something to enjoy on a birthday cake or at Christmas. They need them every day – for their safety and to help them in their work and in their play.

Some of the women in the village realized they could earn some money to help their families and help the rest of the village at the same time. They would make candles! Two organizations helped them. One is the Africa Cooperative Action Trust, who help people in African villages set up businesses. The other is CAFOD, an organization based in Britain. They made sure the women had the money they needed to start their business. Both these organizations believe it is important to help people help themselves. If they had just given the village some candles, they would soon have run out of candles! Now, about fifteen women work every day, making about 210 candles a day, and they sell these at 50p each to other families in the village. The other families know they can buy good candles very easily, and the women are helping to feed and clothe their own families, and pay for such things as medical care and school.

REFLECTION

Organizations such as the two who helped these women know how important it is to listen to other people. They spend a lot of time getting to know people and finding out what they really need. They don't just rush in and give people what they have already decided they need. They listen and learn what will really help them. Do we listen to other people, or are we too busy rushing round?

LINK

Light section, pages 42–55; 'Candlemas', page 18; 'Fair-share Bananas', page 32

Note

Note: This activity is useful in considering changes of matter. The pupils are interested to see the raw materials, and to discuss the changes.

17 Treasure!

You will need

- a world map or a globe
- a Bible (several in different versions if possible)

Introduction

Ask the pupils to think about valuable things. Ask what sort of things are valuable, and what they think is the most valuable thing in their school. Did they all choose the same thing? (Talk about people who are valuable if any of them mention people.) Different people have different ideas about what is valuable. Ask them to think in silence about their most valuable thing at home. They need not tell anyone what it is! Some will probably think about something that would not be at all valuable to other people. There is a book which many people all over the world think is very valuable. But they don't mean it is worth a lot of money! When Queen Elizabeth II was crowned, she was given this book, and told, 'This is the most valuable thing on earth!' She was very rich, and had gold crowns and jewels. She owned several huge houses and castles and a lot of land. But she was told this book was more valuable than all of these things – and many people agreed. The book was the Bible.

Core material

Why is the Bible so valuable to many people? Christians believe the Bible is God's message to them. They believe he made sure everything in it was written down for them to read. They believe he teaches and helps them when they read it. Christians in this country can easily read the Bible. Bibles are for sale in many shops, and many Christians have more than one at home (show any you have available). But some Christians can't get a Bible at all. Perhaps their country does not let them have Bibles, or they cannot afford to buy one. Some Christians cannot read the Bible because there isn't a Bible in their own language. Explain

what a language is. Show Great Britain on the map, and ask how many languages are spoken here (e.g. English, Welsh, Gaelic, Urdu, Punjabi). Then show Africa, and ask how many languages they think it has. Nearly two thousand languages are known in Africa! Many people there cannot read and understand the Bible because it has not yet been written in their own language. Over half of the two thousand African languages do not have their own Bible. Many people are working to translate the Bible into other languages. Some of these work for A.I.M., an organization that helps people in Africa, teaches them about God, and translates the Bible. Here is a story from A.I.M. about a boy called Baraka.

Baraka had been working hard all day. He had brought his family's cows out to the plains to eat fresh grass. He had to watch very carefully for wild animals and to keep the cows safe. It had been a long day. He had just decided to go home when a terrible storm started. The wind nearly blew him over, and the sky became dark with clouds. The storm was so bad that he could not go home. But some people called Paul and Jill saw him. They were living in a village near by to tell people about Jesus and about God's love. They went out into the storm to take Baraka to their home for the night. They made sure the cows were safe too. They told Baraka about Jesus, and he decided to ask Jesus to be his friend. Next day, Baraka waved goodbye and went home. Soon afterwards, Paul and Jill left the village too. Baraka was only ten years old, and now he had no one to tell him more about Jesus. He wished he had something he could read to find out more, but no one had written the Bible in his language. He didn't even know how to read, because he couldn't go to school. But he wanted to stay a friend of Jesus, and he asked Jesus to help him.

Ten years later, Baraka saw Paul and Jill again! They had come back to the village – but this time, they had something with them. They had spent the ten years translating the Bible into Baraka's own language. 'But,' said Baraka, 'I still can't read.' Paul and Jill taught him – and soon he was able to read about God and Jesus by himself. At last, he could read and understand his own Bible!

REFLECTION

Ask the pupils to imagine what it would be like if all their books were in another language. Ask them to think about the book they would miss the most. Many Christians would say that they would miss the Bible the most.

PRAYER

Thank you, God, for books and all the pleasure and help they bring us.

18 Light

Note

The activities in the assemblies in this section (and 'The Lamplighters', page 36) can be used to build up a display on light. This can then be linked with any work on light in other subjects, such as Science or History.

You will need

- two large sheets of paper as backing sheets for the posters, one entitled 'Where does our light come from?', the other 'Why do we need light?'
- pieces of paper, cut to an appropriate size for inclusion on the posters
- pencils/crayons
- scissors
- a candle and matches
- glue

Introduction

Ask the pupils where the light in your hall/room is coming from. Unless it is a dull day, most of the light will probably be coming through the windows. Where does this light come from? If you met here in the late evening, where would the light come from then? Would there be enough light coming through the windows? Ask the pupils who gave you the answers to these questions to come to the front and draw each light source for you twice – on two separate pieces of paper.

Explain that together you are going to make a poster showing all the sources of light people use or have used in the past. Choose two pupils to stick one of each finished drawing onto the first sheet. The pupils can continue drawing and assembling the poster while you continue. Ask them to sit down quietly at the front when they finish their own picture. Ask for further examples of light sources, and ask each pupil to draw the source they name, twice (as above). Help them to include such things as street lamps, candles, torches, and oil lamps.

There is one source of light which is there every day, of course: the sun. Ask the pupils to think for a few minutes about what would happen if we did not have any of the other sources of light. What sort of things would we not be able to do? What would happen at night-time? Encourage them to discuss why we need light every day and night. As each use of light is mentioned, discuss it and write the appropriate sentence from the list below onto the second poster. Ask which sources of light should be stuck onto the poster under each sentence. Some pictures might need drawing again. If any sentence has not been suggested, help the pupils to think about it. Add any they have thought of for themselves.

- Light helps us to be safe.
- Light shows us the way to go.
- Light helps us to be healthy.
- Light helps plants to grow.
- Light helps us to work and to play.

REFLECTION

Light the candle and ask the pupils to think about the difference light makes to our lives.

LINK

'The Lamplighters', page 36; 'Dipping and Making Candles', page 38; 'Candlemas', page 18

19 Jesus, the Light of the World

You will need

- the posters entitled 'Why do we need light?' and 'Where does our light come from?' from the previous assembly.

Introduction

Jesus said that he was the Light of the World. We have drawn many things which give us light – but none of them are people! So what did Jesus mean when he said this? Here are some of the ways in which Jesus is like a light for the people who follow him.

Light shows us the way to go.

Christians believe that Jesus shows them the way to go – he shows them how to live and what to do. They believe that, if they follow what he says to them, they will live as he wants them to. This is one of the ways in which he keeps them safe.

Light helps to keep us safe.

Christians believe that Jesus loves them and that he looks after them all the time. This does not mean that they will never be in danger or never be hurt. The danger is still there, but Christians believe that Jesus will be with them and that he will never leave them. (The assembly on page 48 shows one way in which Jesus keeps his friends safe. Refer to this if appropriate.)

Light helps plants to grow.

This doesn't mean that Jesus' friends – Christians – are much taller than other people! As we grow up, we get taller, but we grow in other ways, too. We learn how to do more and more things. Ask the pupils to think for a minute about the things they can do now that they couldn't do when they were a baby. As we grow up, we learn about more things too. Ask them to think about something they are learning about at the moment that they didn't know about last year, or even last week. As we grow up, we also learn more about how we should behave. Christians believe that Jesus is teaching them all the time: he teaches them how they should treat others, and he teaches them how to do new things. Most importantly, they believe that he teaches them how to obey and follow God. So they are growing in these ways all the time.

Light helps us to be healthy.

Christians do not believe that Jesus keeps them healthy all the time. They might catch measles or break their legs, just as anyone else might! But Christians believe that Jesus helps them to be healthy inside. He helps them to do the right thing and to obey God. He helps them to get rid of the feelings that make them miserable, such as jealousy and hatred.

PRAYER

Thank you, Jesus, that you are like a light to your friends. Thank you that you show them how to live and help them to enjoy life.

LINK

'Candlemas', page 18 – this is the festival on which Christians traditionally celebrate Jesus being welcomed into the Temple as a baby.

20 The Bible as a Light

You will need

- the poster entitled 'Why do we need light?' (see page 42)
- a torch with a strong beam
- a sheet of paper
- felt-tips

Introduction

We have been looking at the uses of light. Remind the pupils of the uses listed on their poster. Footballers use a special kind of lights. Do any of the pupils know what sort and why? Talk about the use of floodlights to enable matches to continue in dull weather and in the evening. Draw a simple representation of a floodlight in the middle of one side of the paper, and a beam of light spreading out from it, so that it covers the whole of the other side of the paper. Would the lights be any good if they only showed the players the ground just in front of them? What else do footballers need to see during a match? (Other players and the goals.) Would the lights be any good if they just showed the two goals and nothing else, so that the ground in between the two goals was always in darkness? The floodlights have to show the players where they are running – the ground beneath their feet – and also the whole of the pitch, so that they know where they are running to.

Christians believe the Bible is like those floodlights at a football pitch. There is a verse in the Bible which says, 'Your word (the Bible) is a lamp to my feet and a light for my path.' (Psalm 119.105) Talk about a light shining on your feet and on your path further away. Christians believe that this verse means the Bible does two things: it shows them what they should do and how they should behave at the moment, just as the floodlight shows the player's next step. They believe the Bible also shows what they should do in the future, just as the floodlight shows the whole of the pitch. So the Bible shows Christians how to behave every day, and also how to behave in the future. This means they can know what God wants them to do each day, and also know what God wants them to aim for in the future – just as football players know where it is safe to run, and can see the goal and aim for it.

Christians believe that if they read the Bible it will tell them what God wants them to do and how he wants them to live. There are many things in the Bible which God wants them to do. Jesus once said that the most important thing his friends should do was this: 'Love God, and love other people just as you love yourself.' He meant that if his friends did this, they would be doing the other things too, because they would be living as God wants them to live. Write this verse in the light from the floodlight on the paper.

REFLECTION

Use the torch's beam to illustrate the following:

As we live our lives, we need to know what to do each day (shine beam at your feet) and what to do in the future – what we should be aiming at (shine beam ahead of you). Ask the pupils to think about these two things – what they want to do today and what they want to do in the future. Christians believe that reading God's word shows them both of these things.

LINK

'We Are Marching in the Light of God', page 100

21 Lighthouses – Danger!

You will need

- the poster entitled 'Why do we need light?' (see page 42)

Introduction

Ask the pupils what a lighthouse is. Where do we see them? Why are they there? Usually, it is to warn ships of dangers – ask what these dangers might be (currents or hidden rocks). Why do ships need to be warned about these things? How do lighthouses warn the sailors? Talk about the light that warns sailors. Lighthouses are there to keep people safe. Lighthouses have to be placed very carefully, so that their light can be seen clearly by the sailors and so that they see it early enough to change course. It is no good seeing the light after they have crashed into the rocks.

Over two hundred years ago, people decided they needed a lighthouse on the north Cheshire coast. They chose the ideal place to build the lighthouse – but then things went wrong. The soil was so sandy they could not build strong enough foundations for the tall lighthouse walls. They didn't know what to do. Then someone decided to use something very unusual. A ship carrying cotton from America had been wrecked. The great bundles of fluffy cotton had been soaked by the sea. The people carried this cotton to the spot where they wanted to build the lighthouse, and put it all into the hole they had dug. The cotton was soaked with water and very hard. They built the walls on top of this – and the lighthouse is still standing, over two hundred years later!

Christians would say the Bible is like a lighthouse for them. They mean that the Bible can keep them safe. A lighthouse warns people there is danger ahead. It tells the sailors which way they should go to avoid the danger. The danger is still there, but the sailors know how to keep themselves safe from it. Ask the pupils what could happen if the sailors saw the lighthouse, and said, 'That means there are rocks over there which might make a hole in our ship. Never mind, we'll be all right if we just carry on.' A warning only works if people listen to it and believe it is telling the truth. Christians believe the Bible tells them some things are dangerous. Some things will hurt people – themselves and others. So Christians try not to do those things. The pupils may have talked about some of the things which can hurt people in the assembly on Lent (page 16). Talk briefly about two of these now.

Add a lighthouse to the light sources poster if necessary. Then add to the other poster, under the heading 'Light keeps us safe':

- a picture of the Bible, and
- the sentence 'Christians believe the Bible helps keep them safe.'

PRAYER

Thank you, God, that your book warns people of danger because you do not want them to hurt themselves or other people. Thank you that people can trust those warnings.

REFLECTION

Ask the pupils to consider whether they always listen to warnings. Sometimes we do not understand why someone is warning us about something – just as sailors might not see any rocks and wonder why the lighthouse is there. We have to trust the people who are warning us, just as the sailors trust the lighthouse.

22

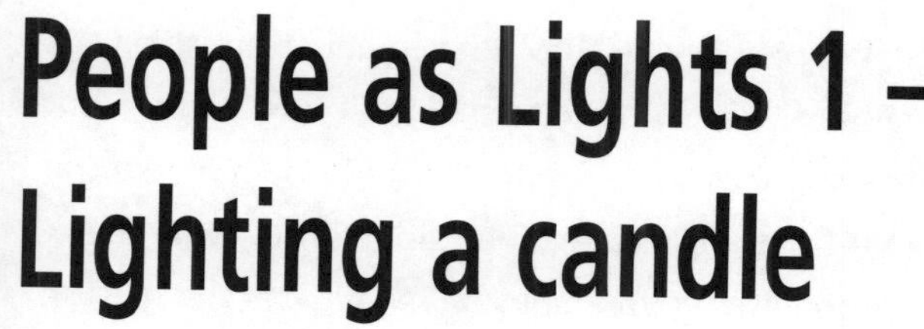

People as Lights 1 – Lighting a candle

You will need

- a candle and matches

Introduction

Tell or read this story to the pupils:

It was seven o'clock in the evening and it was dark outside. It was dark inside, too, because the electricity was off. Mr Brown was with three of his children. They were all annoyed.

'I can't see to read the report about the football match!' said Mr Brown.

'I can't see to finish my comic!' said Megan.

'I can't see to finish my story for school!' said Harry.

'I can't see to finish eating my cake!' said Nathan.

Everyone was quiet for a moment. Then Mr Brown said, 'Why can't you finish eating your cake, Nathan? You don't have to see to eat it!'

Nathan said, 'But I don't know where I put it! I can't find it!'

Matthew arrived home. 'Why is it so dark in here?' he asked, and they told him about the electricity. 'Then why don't you light a candle?' he said. He felt his way over to the cupboard, and found the candles and the matches. He lit two candles – and the whole family could see what they were doing again. 'Oh dear!' said Matthew. 'I think I've trodden in some cake!'

The whole family complained about the darkness – but only Matthew did something about it. There is a saying, 'It is better to light a candle than to complain about the darkness.' This saying isn't about real darkness like a power cut, and real light, like that from candles. It means something more difficult to understand. Things don't always go right. Sometimes we are sad, angry or lonely. We often see other people who are unhappy. It is easy to say, 'Yes, it's terrible that those people have been treated unfairly.' But just saying that doesn't do any good. People need to do what they can to help these people. That is what the saying means. It is no good just complaining about things. We have to try to change things as well.

Of course, not everyone can help others, no matter how much they want to. We should never feel guilty when we see others who need help if we can't do anything to help them. But there are small ways in which we can all help. If we see someone in school being treated unfairly, we can tell someone. (You may want to talk about the school's anti-bullying policy here.) If we see that someone is unhappy, we can talk to them. Sometimes even schoolchildren can make a difference. One school wrote letters to their local council because a new building estate was going to destroy a pond where rare animals lived. The council read the letters and made sure that the pond was safe when the new houses were built. The children of that school could just have said, 'It's a shame, but we can't do anything.' But they decided to try – and they succeeded. They didn't just complain about something, they did something. It was like lighting a candle.

REFLECTION

Light a candle and ask the pupils to look at it while you read the following:

We see many things that make us angry and unhappy. We know we can't do anything about most of them. Some of us are too young. Some of us don't have any power. But sometimes, there is something we can do. Sometimes, we can help the people who are sad. Sometimes, we can tell someone else who does have some power. Sometimes, we can light a candle to make life easier for other people.

LINK

'We Are Marching in the Light of God', page 100; 'Daniel', page 24; 'Fair-share Bananas', page 32; 'The Lamplighters', page 36; 'St. Brigid's Cross', page 44

23 People as Lights 2 – Light or dark?

You will need

- a box of bricks

Introduction

Ask the pupils to retell the story of the Brown family and the power cut. Prompt them to include an account of the family's feelings throughout the story. Sometimes, other people can be like that darkness. Other people can make us feel miserable and unhappy. Sometimes, people say cruel things to us, and make us unhappy. Sometimes, people won't share things with us. Ask the pupils if they can think of any other ways in which other people can make us miserable and stop us from feeling happy.

When Matthew lit the candles, the Brown family felt happier. They were able to get on with what they wanted to do. Matthew helped them, and the light helped them. In the same way, sometimes other people can make us happy. They can help us do what we have to do, and help us feel less frightened of something. Ask the pupils if they can think of any other ways in which other people can help us to feel happy. These people are like the light in the story. They cheer us up, just as light cheers us up on a dark, gloomy evening.

It isn't just other people who can be like darkness or light. We can all be like darkness and light, too! We can make people feel happier because they met us, or more miserable! Ask the pupils to think in silence about how they have made people feel today. Perhaps they have made someone feel happy. Perhaps they have made someone feel miserable. Sometimes, it is very easy to make someone feel happy or sad. It can take something as simple as a frown to make someone feel miserable. Ask the pupils to frown. Then ask them to show on their faces what the opposite of this would be, something that would make other people feel happier. Sometimes, the way in which we say something can make someone happy or miserable. Say 'Hello!' as if you wish you hadn't met the person, then ask them to show you how they would say 'Hello!' if they were pleased to see the person. Sometimes, the way in which we do things makes people feel happy or miserable. Scatter the bricks on the floor, and ask one pupil to pick them up as if they are happy to do this, and another to do it as if they don't want to and would rather be playing outside. Even if we help someone, we can still make them feel unhappy by the way we do the job!

Ask the pupils to think about this as they go through the day. We can be like light and make people feel better, or we can be like darkness and make people feel miserable. Jesus was thinking of this when he told his followers that they should be like light to other people. He was saying that they should try to make life easier and happier for others, and not make people miserable by what they did or said.

REFLECTION

Ask the pupils to close their eyes and to think about a time when they know they made someone unhappy. Then ask them to think about a time when they know they made someone happy. Ask them to look out for a chance to make someone feel better today. But remind them no one can be perfect all the time! We all have days when we feel miserable ourselves, and when other people annoy us!

LINK

'Daniel', page 24; 'The Lamplighters', page 36; *Lent* section, pages 14–17

24 A Letter and a Crocodile! Royal Sailors' Rests

Introduction

Over a hundred years ago, a woman called Agnes Weston lived in Bath. Many young boys went there to join the Army. They were away from home, and had few friends. Agnes started a coffee shop for them, so they would have somewhere safe and comfortable to meet together. Often, they were sent to countries far away from Britain. Few had anyone to write to them, because many of their parents couldn't write. Agnes realized how lonely they were, and she promised to write to them. One day, a sailor saw a soldier reading one of these letters. They were on a ship called H.M.S. *Crocodile*. He asked for Agnes' address and wrote to her, asking her to write to him, too. Soon, she was writing to many sailors who lived lonely and dangerous lives.

Some other sailors asked Agnes if she would open a house in Devonport in Plymouth, where many of the Navy ships stayed when they were in Britain. She agreed, and her friend Sophia Wintz helped her. Many sailors were soon visiting this house. It was somewhere they could meet together and enjoy their time ashore. Soon, Agnes had started other Rests, as they were called, in other towns and cities, wherever the sailors needed her. These Rests are still operating today, including one at a submarine base. They are often called 'Aggies', from Agnes' name. The people who work there do many things to help sailors and their families. Often, sailors stay there when there is not time for them to travel long distances to their homes.The helpers run playgroups for sailors' children, and some have gyms where sailors' wives can keep fit. Some of these women are alone for many long weeks while their husbands are at sea. The Aggies provide somewhere they can meet together, as well as help in looking after the children. The Aggies welcome anyone who needs their help. And there is always someone at the Rests who can help people learn more about God if they want to.

Many people are helped each year by these houses. But it all started when one woman decided to help one person. The newsletters which the organization sends out used to have a lighthouse on the front. Discuss why the lighthouse is an appropriate logo for this organization. The lighthouse shows sailors where it is safe to sail their ships. In the same way, the houses started by Agnes Weston show sailors and their families a place where they can be safe and where they can enjoy themselves. A lighthouse helps sailors, and the people who work at the Rests are always ready to help sailors too.

REFLECTION

Agnes Weston did not start off with several big buildings and many people helping her. She started off with just one letter, sent to someone who was lonely. We don't have to do a lot to help others. Just one little thing can make them feel happier.

LINK

'People as Lights', pages 50 and 52

25 I Spy

You will need

- a range of articles in shades of one colour, e.g. green
- a painting in which perspective is used, so that far objects/people appear to be smaller than those in the foreground
- a large sheet of paper on which pairs of letters are randomly arranged
- pencils

Introduction

Play a game of I Spy with the pupils – either between them and yourself, or between two teams. Set a time limit for the game, and make sure other limits of the game are clear to all before the start: i.e. only articles visible in the room are to be used; only five guesses for each article will be allowed. Afterwards, ask the pupils to tell you some of the articles they could use in various settings, e.g. at the seaside, in the country, in the main street. Talk about how we take being able to see all these things for granted, and how different life would be if we couldn't see them.

Note

In this series of assemblies on 'Sight', sensitivity needs to be exercised if there is a pupil or an adult with sight impairment or loss in the group or school. Individual teachers who know the person concerned will be best able to judge which parts – if any – of these assemblies should be used.

As well as just seeing things, our eyes tell us a lot of other things too.

When we look at something, our eyes can tell us what colour something is. They do not just tell us that something is green or blue, they also tell us that some things are different shades of the same colour. Show the pupils the objects in different shades of a colour, and ask for two volunteers to put them in order, the palest at one end. Ask the pupils for some of the words we use to describe shades of colours, such as pale, deep, light. Many of these different shades have their own names. Talk about sky blue, navy blue, royal blue, showing examples of any you can see.

When we look at things, our eyes can also tell us which is furthest away from us. Show the pupils the perspective picture, to explain what you mean. When we see things in the distance, they look small; but we know they are not really small. It is just because we are a long way from them. Talk about what people look like if we look down from a high building, or from an aeroplane.

Our eyes can also see tiny differences between small things, such as letters. Ask some of the youngest pupils to draw lines between the pairs of letters on the paper. If our eyes could not tell these differences, we could not learn to read or write!

Ask the pupils to suggest other things our eyes can do.

PRAYER

If appropriate, invite the pupils to contribute their own colours, etc. at the points marked *:

Thank you, Father, for all the things our eyes can do. Thank you for all the colours we see. Thank you for our favourite colours:*
Thank you for the things we can see in the countryside. Thank you for*
Thank you for the things we can see in town. Thank you for *.
Thank you for the books we can read. Thank you for*.
Thank you for everything we can see.

26 The Woman's Gift

Note

This assembly is closely based upon one used by a teacher of visually impaired pupils. It is intended to follow on from the 'I Spy' assembly. Sensitivity needs to be exercised if there is a pupil or an adult with hearing impairment in the group or school.

You will need

- a large opaque mixing bowl, deep enough for your hand to be hidden as you release coins in it
- coins – individual £1, 50p, 20p, and 1p coins; two 1p coins; a handful of assorted change

Introduction

Recap on the assembly about the information our eyes give us. It talked about our eyes being able to see small differences between things. We use this ability when we go shopping. Talk about why we need to tell the difference between different coins. But people who cannot see well cannot use this method of telling which coin is which. Ask the pupils if they can think of any other way in which we can tell one coin from another – a way which people who could not see well could use (touch). Ask some pupils to close their eyes and give them a £1 coin and a 50p coin and ask them to tell the others which is which. People who cannot see well use this method a lot. The designers of coins have to think about this when they design new coins. There is another way of telling which coin is which, and that is by listening to it!

LINK

This assembly can be linked with ***The Senses: Hearing*** section in Book 1 and the ***Taste*** section in Book 3 of this series.

This is an assembly which a teacher used when she taught children who could not see as well as the pupils can. (You may need to alter this statement.) Ask the pupils to close their eyes and listen carefully while you drop various coins into the bowl. Explain that you do not expect them to be perfect at this! Go through the individual coins, and end by making sure they know what a 1p coin sounds like. Tell them they will be hearing this again in the story. Then tell the following story, dropping the coins into the bowl as indicated.

Jesus was once teaching in part of the Temple, where people came to pray and to worship God. There was a huge bowl nearby, where people brought the money they wanted to give to the Temple. Jesus watched the rich people. They dropped a lot of coins into the bowl (drop in the handful of coins), and the coins made a lot of noise! Then a woman came. Her clothes were old and Jesus and his friends could tell she did not have much money. She walked up to the bowl, and dropped in just two very small coins (drop in the two 1p coins separately). Ask the pupils which coins they think these were, and then show them. The 1p is the lowest value coin we now have, and the woman gave the smallest coins they had at that time.

Jesus said, 'This woman has given more than all those rich people did. They gave a lot, but they have plenty more money at home. But she has given all the money she has.'

Jesus said the woman had shown how much she loved God because she gave so generously to God's Temple.

REFLECTION

Probably most of the people at the assembly today find it easy to tell which coin is which, and to choose what they want to buy. But even something like this becomes very difficult for the people whose eyesight is not as good as ours. Drop the coins in again, one at a time, and ask the pupils to think about the people who need to use their other senses – hearing and touch – to be able to go shopping.

If time allows, also use this Reflection:

It is easy to be generous when we have a lot, but it is not so easy when we do not have much to give. A gift does not have to be worth a lot of money to be valuable to the person who receives it. Ask the pupils to tell you about gifts that do not cost a lot of money – a gift of time, for instance, if a younger brother wants to play with them when they would rather be doing something else. Then ask them to think quietly about gifts they could give to other people that would mean a lot to them.

27 The Man who Came Through the Roof

Introduction

Ask the pupils to show you with their hands the shape of their roof. Comment on the shapes. Ask them what the roofs are made of. Do they know what roofs are made of in other countries? Talk about roofs made of branches or leaves (refer to banana leaves if the assembly on page 28 has been used), and roofs made of mud – and of all of these together. What shape would roofs be if they were made of these things? Jesus lived in a house with a flat roof made of mud and branches. The house had just one storey (explain as necessary) and the people living in it slept on the roof in hot weather, and kept things on it. So they built a staircase leading up to the roof. One day, a man went through a roof like this – but he didn't fall! Here is what happened.

Core material

Jesus had come to Capernaum, and a lot of people wanted to see him. They wanted to hear him talking about God. They had heard how interesting he was to listen to and that he told wonderful stories. Some of them had also heard he had made ill people better, and they wanted to ask him to help them. But one man (we'll call him Matt) could not go by himself, although he wanted to. Matt couldn't walk at all. He spent all day every day lying on his bed. His bed wasn't like your beds. It was just a thin mattress on the floor. Every day, his friends came and carried him on this bed into the streets. There, he would ask the people passing by to give him some money so he could buy food. So when his friends came into his house, Matt thought they were just taking him out as usual. But instead, they told him they were taking him to see Jesus! He was very excited. 'Perhaps Jesus will make me better!' he thought. But when they arrived at the house where Jesus was teaching, his friends put down Matt's bed.

'We're sorry,' they said, 'but there isn't room in there for you. It is too crowded!' Matt was very disappointed – and his friends knew he was. One of them said, 'We can't just give up like this. I know what we can do. We'll go up onto the roof and make a hole in it, and lower Matt down on his bed.' And that is just what they did. They borrowed some tools and dug through the mud. They tore away the branches and made a hole big enough for the bed. Then they tied strong rope onto the corners of the bed, and lowered Matt down into the house. It felt funny, swaying through the air, but Matt didn't care. He was so pleased to be near to Jesus.

The people in the house couldn't believe it when mud started to fall on them. Was the roof falling in, they wondered? They looked up, and saw the bed! Down and down it came, until it reached the floor – right in front of Jesus! Jesus looked up, and saw the friends looking down at him. He knew what they wanted and why they had gone to so much trouble. He looked down at Matt and said, 'Pick up your bed – and walk home!' And Matt did just that. Everyone watched in amazement as Matt stood up, picked up the bed and walked out of the house. Most of the people knew him and knew he could not walk. But here he was, walking as well as they could. The friends on the roof were so pleased that they cheered, and people thanked God for the wonderful thing they had just seen.

PRAYER

Thank you, Jesus, that you cared about people like the friends and Matt. Thank you that you care about people today. Thank you that other people help each other today, just as the friends helped Matt.

REFLECTION

The friends did not give up easily, even when things were difficult. Ask the pupils to think about themselves – do they give up easily, or do they keep on trying when things are hard to do?

LINK

'Abraham', page 20; 'The Girl', page 64; 'The Man who Said Thank You', page 68

28 The Terrible Storm – Fear and peace (a whole-class assembly)

You will need

- a P.E. bench or long table, laid on its side to represent a boat, at the front, but to one side: disciples sit behind this in two rows, ready to row; Jesus sits at the back
- parts in the mime allocated to a whole class: Jesus, twelve disciples, the crowd. Stress that none of them have any words to say. If they listen carefully as you read the story, they will be able to follow your 'instructions'.

Introduction

Ask the pupils to show a range of feelings on their faces (such as anger, happiness, worry), and then ask them to suggest and demonstrate some more. Sometimes, it is not just our faces that show our feelings. Sometimes, our whole body shows people how we are feeling. Show how you would walk if you were really tired, or if you were very angry. Ask pupils to demonstrate other examples if they can think of any, or suggest happiness, worry, a feeling of relaxation.

In this story from the Bible, Jesus' special friends, the disciples, felt strong feelings that changed very quickly! Ask your 'actors' to take up their positions – the crowd and disciples are listening to Jesus, who is teaching them. Pause at the points marked * in the story, to allow the 'actors' time to perform each action.

One day, Jesus had been teaching a large crowd of people for a long time.* He was tired.* He and his disciples got into a boat* and the disciples started to row across the lake.* Jesus settled down in the back of the boat and went to sleep.* The crowd waved goodbye*, and then set off home.* Suddenly, a terrible storm swept across the water. The boat rocked* and the disciples tried very hard to row to the shore.* But they couldn't.* One of them went over to Jesus and woke him up.* The disciple pointed at the huge waves*.

'Don't you care that we are going to drown?' he shouted.

Jesus looked around.* He stood up* and held his arms out over the water.* 'Be quiet!' he said to the wind. 'Be still!' he said to the waves. And the wind stopped. The water became peaceful once more.

The disciples were amazed.* They asked each other* who Jesus could be, for even the wind and the waves did as he told them.

Ask the pupils what the disciples would be feeling at each stage of this story. Invite them to tell the 'actors' what feelings they should be showing when, and ask the 'actors' to show the others how they would show these feelings. Then repeat the story and mime, asking the actors to reflect these feelings.

REFLECTION

Christians believe that Jesus is still with them when they are feeling frightened or worried. They believe he can turn those feelings into feelings of peace.

29 The Girl – Sadness and joy

Introduction

Some people find it easy to ask for help when they need it. Many people don't find it easy! A lot of pupils get this sentence written on their reports: 'They must ask for help when they need it!' We may find it difficult to ask for help, but usually when we do pluck up our courage and ask for help, people are very happy to help us in any way they can. In this story from the Bible, one man came and asked for help from Jesus, but one woman did not dare ask for help. Jesus helped them both!

(**NB** At this point, teachers may like to speak about not approaching strangers, and discuss with pupils who we should ask for help.)

Jairus hurried through the street. How he hoped he would be in time! He saw the crowds as soon as he was near the shore of the lake. He pushed his way through, and, at last, he was next to Jesus. He knelt down in front of him, and said, 'Please, Jesus, come home with me. My daughter is ill – so ill that the doctors say she is dying.' Jesus said he would come straight away. Jairus pointed out which way to go, and hurried off with him as the disciples followed behind.

The crowd came too! They wanted to be with Jesus for as long as they could. There was a woman in the crowd who had been ill for many years. Many doctors had tried to help her, but no one could. She had heard of Jesus and of the wonderful things he was doing. She had heard how he had healed a man who suffered from leprosy and a man who couldn't walk.

'Jesus won't want to be bothered with me,' she thought. 'If I could just touch his clothes, I believe I would be healed, too.' So she pushed through the crowd until she was next to Jesus, and she reached out and touched the edge of his clothes.

Immediately, she knew she was healed! But before she could creep away, Jesus stopped and said, 'Someone touched me! Who was it?'

The disciples said that many people were bumping into Jesus as they all tried to walk through the narrow streets. But Jesus meant that someone had touched him for healing. Then the woman stepped forward and told Jesus what she had done. He told her that she had been healed because she had believed he could heal her.

While Jesus spoke to the woman, some of Jairus' servants came and told him that his daughter was dead. Jesus said, 'Don't be frightened, Jairus. Just believe in me.' Then Jesus told three of his disciples – Peter, James and John – to come with him, and they hurried on to Jairus' home.

People there were already crying and weeping for the dead girl. Jesus told them to stop, and he went into the house. There, he bent down and held the girl's hand. 'Get up now,' he said – and the girl opened her eyes, stretched, and sat up. Her parents were overjoyed. 'Don't tell anyone else what has happened,' Jesus said. 'Your daughter is hungry – get her some food!' Then he and his disciples left the family together.

PRAYER

Invite the pupils to contribute to this prayer:

Thank you, God, that we have so many people to help us in this country.
Thank you for nurses, doctors and all the other people who work to make us feel better.
Thank you for ... .

LINK

Easter section, page 80; 'Abraham', page 20; 'The Man who Came Through the Roof', page 60

30 The Boy's Packed Lunch – A whole-class assembly

Note

This assembly is to be followed by the music assembly 'The Feeding of the Five Thousand' on page 104.

You will need

- a child's lunch box
- (optional) five plastic bread rolls and two plastic fish inside lunch box
- a list of the school meal/s available on this day

Introduction

[To prepare for this assembly, allocate roles: boy with lunch box; Jesus (or describe Jesus' actions instead); a few disciples; the rest of the class as the crowd. Read through the 'play' with the pupils once, so they know their actions.]

Ask the pupils what they would do if they were out for the day with their family or friends, and they were hungry. Discuss the places selling food or meals. If they knew they were going to a place which was miles away from any shops or cafés, what could they do? Talk about the sort of food and drinks they like to pack up if they are going out for the day. Let's find out what the pupils will be eating today. Tell them what today's school dinner/s is/are, giving the 'dinner pupils' time to make a choice if necessary. Then ask the 'packed-lunch pupils' to think about the contents of their lunch boxes. Do any of the 'home pupils' know what they will be eating? Then ask how many of the pupils will be eating some bread today. Discuss what form this will be in. How many of them will be eating fish? Discuss what forms this might come in. Will any of them be having just bread and fish, and nothing else?

There is a story in the Bible about a young boy who set off to work in the fields with his normal lunch – just five small rolls of bread and two small fishes. What he didn't know was that he would finish up sharing this lunch with thousands of other people!

One day, Jesus was tired. He went across the lake in a boat. *Jesus walks over to one side of the 'stage'.*

But a lot of people walked round the lake to join him. *Some of the crowd follow him.* In fact, thousands of people followed him! *The rest join him.*

They wanted to hear him teaching them again about God and about his love for them. *Crowd sits down ready to listen.*

Jesus talked to the people for a long time. It got later and later. *Some of crowd yawn and stretch.*

The crowd were very hungry. *Crowd rub their tummies and say, 'We're starving!'*

The disciples asked Jesus what they should do. *Disciples come up to Jesus.*

Jesus said, 'You give them some food!' *Jesus points at them.*

Most of the disciples said, 'We haven't got any food!' *All the disciples except one hold out empty hands or show their pockets are empty.*

But one disciple said, 'This boy has some food!' *The boy with his lunch box joins the disciple.*

The boy opens it (and holds up the food). 'I have five little loaves and two fishes,' the boy said.

Jesus took the food and said thank you to God for it. Then he broke it up and gave it to the disciples. *Jesus pretends to do this.*

The disciples took the food to everyone in the crowd. *Disciples give the food to everyone.*

The crowd enjoyed their meal. The bread was fresh and the fish was delicious. *Crowd make appreciative faces and noises!*

Afterwards, the disciples picked up all the bits that were left – twelve baskets full! *The disciples go round picking up food, and then pretend to carry heavy baskets off the stage.*

Everyone went home happy and full! *Crowd walks off happily.*

REFLECTION

Ask the pupils to imagine that they are the boy, and to imagine what they would have said to their parents when they arrived home after the gigantic picnic!

LINK

'The Feeding of the Five Thousand', page 104

31 The Man who Said Thank You

You will need

- the information about leprosy between asterisks on pages 36–37

Introduction

Ask the pupils to think about what might happen when they go to see the doctor. Ask whether the doctor might say each of these things:

- 'I know what the matter is with you. I'll give you some medicine.'
- 'You've sprained your ankle. I'll bandage it up.'
- 'I'm not sure why your shoulder is hurting, so I'll send you for an x-ray at the hospital.'
- 'I don't want other people to catch what you've got, so you must leave home at once and live in a field a long way away from everyone else.'

Ask the pupils how they'd feel if the doctor said the last thing! Of course, no doctor would say that to any of them! But once, doctors said that quite often! If they thought someone had a disease called leprosy, doctors would not give them any medicine or tablets. Instead, they would say (read out last item again). If the assembly about leprosy (pages 36–37) has been used, refer to this now, and remind the pupils about the old beliefs about the disease and modern knowledge about it. If not, introduce and read the information between asterisks on pages 36–37.

This is a story from the Bible about what happened to one group of people who had to leave home because they had leprosy.

No one wanted to go near someone who had leprosy. They were too frightened of catching the disease themselves. So the ten men with leprosy lived up in the hills, in a cave. They had left their families and friends back at home. Sometimes they came down the hillside to stand near the road. They would shout to people walking along the road, asking them to throw some money or food to them. Sometimes their families and friends were able to leave them some food at the side of the road, but they never came close to them.

Then one day a crowd of people came along the road. 'What's happening?' one of the men shouted, and someone told them that Jesus was coming. They had heard about Jesus and how he had healed many people who had been ill. 'Perhaps he could help us!' one of the men said.

'There he is!' another man said. Then they all shouted, 'Jesus, please help us!'

Jesus stopped. He looked at the ten men, ill and dressed in rags. 'Go to the priests,' he shouted to them. Now, the men knew that if they were ever healed they would have to see the priests before they would be allowed to return to their homes.

They hurried off – and as they went, they realized that they had been healed. Their skin was healthy once more. They no longer had leprosy! Nine of them hurried on, but one stopped. He turned round – and hurried back to Jesus. He pushed through the crowd, and knelt in front of Jesus. 'Thank you!' he said. 'Thank you for healing me!'

Jesus asked, 'Where are the others? All ten were healed. Where are they?' Then he said to the man, 'You are healed because you believed I could help you. Go to the priests now, and then you can go home to your family.' And the man hurried off. He could hardly wait to see his family again.

REFLECTION

We think now that people used to be very cruel in the way they treated people with leprosy, even though they were afraid of catching the disease. People today can still be cruel in the way they treat others. Ask the pupils to think carefully about how they treat other people. Are they less than kind to some people just because others tell them to treat them like that?

LINK

'The Lamplighters', page 36; 'Abraham', page 20; 'The Girl', page 64

32 Stone Carvings – An elephant with the wrong ears!

Note

These assemblies are designed for use in conjunction with a visit to a church. The choice of assembly and of material within an assembly will depend upon the denomination (and age) of church visited. Teachers can decide if an assembly should precede or follow the visit. Either way, the relevant features should be pointed out at the visit, so that the pupils can make the connection between the building and the assemblies. The assemblies could also be used if appropriate illustrations of each feature could be displayed. The use of music in worship can be illustrated by using one of the Music Assemblies. Pupils will probably see a Bible in church, and its value to Christians can be shown using the assembly 'Treasure!', page 40. Another feature of Christian churches which they will see is crosses; the Crosses section can be used, especially the first assembly, on page 92. The Church Visit Assemblies can be linked with the assembly on Mother Church, page 12. Each assembly can be introduced by some of the pupils with an appropriate sentence based on either: 'When we visited ... church, we saw a ...'; or: 'We will see ... when we visit ... church.'

You will need

- (if possible) a selection of leaves from the list in the text (not to be touched by pupils)
- a selection of fruit with which the pupils are familiar
- an unusual fruit they may not know, such as a star fruit or lychee
- pencils and paper
- an enlarged picture of the drawing of the elephant (page 116)

Introduction

Make sure the leaves and unusual fruit are hidden. Invite some pupils to draw one of these each: a banana, an orange, an apple; ask others to draw an elephant, a cat and a dog. Then ask if anyone can draw the unusual fruit you have obtained. If no one can, how the fruit, then ask someone to draw them. Show the others the results, asking each 'artist' if it was easy to draw their object. Then ask the pupils who drew the rarer fruit if it was easy to draw once they saw the fruit.

Core material

The people who built the churches and cathedrals many years ago wanted to make them as beautiful as they could. They used stone for the walls, parts of the ceilings, the columns which supported the weight of the walls and ceilings, and sometimes the floor. They also used stone for decoration. If you visited a church with carved stonework, talk about the subjects of the carving. The people who carved the stone into blocks for the walls, or into decoration, were called stonemasons. The most important ones, who had worked with stone for years, were called Master Masons. Then there were many others learning how to carve. They would be asked to carve things like fruit and animals or patterns and leaves, just as the pupils were asked to draw them. Sometimes they would be asked to carve something they knew well, such as leaves. They could go out into the fields and find the leaves they wanted. Southwell Minster in Nottinghamshire is famous for its very fine carvings of leaves. They include leaves from the hawthorn, oak, elder, ivy and holly trees, which the stonemasons could have seen every day in the nearby forests. (Show any you have been able to obtain, or just mention ivy and holly, which they will probably know.)

But sometimes, stonemasons were asked to carve things which they had never seen. A stonemason in Ottery St. Mary in Devon was asked to carve an elephant. But he had never seen an elephant. He had heard stories about them, and knew their ears were unusual. So he carved an animal with a trunk, tusks – and huge human ears! Nowadays, we all know just what an elephant looks like, and we know that this stonemason got it wrong. Some churches have wild animals such as wolves and wild boars in their carvings. This tells us these animals were still to be seen wild in this country when the churches were built. Now, they can only be seen here in zoos.

So the stonemasons' carvings tell us two things. They tell us what the stonemasons knew and what they didn't know! Ask the pupils what they would do if they were stonemasons working today and had to make carvings of animals they had never seen. Discuss the possible sources of information they could use. More and more of us now can travel abroad as well, and can see the animals and plants that belong in other countries for ourselves.

PRAYER

Ask the pupils to think about all the ways in which we can find out about anything that interests us now. Ask them to listen as you read the prayer:

Thank you, God, for books,
for computers and the Internet,
for films and television,
for teachers and writers,
and for all the ways in which we can learn what we want or need to know.

33 Stained-glass Windows

Note

See note on page 70.

You will need

- a book from school's reading scheme, or 'big book': choose a cover and a page in which the pictures convey a lot of information
- a technical book, such as a car manual, in which the diagrams are vital
- (if possible) a glass decorated with glass paints
- an outline of an arched window, on a flip chart, for instance (see page 116)
- felt-tips

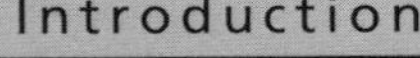

Introduction

Talk about how we obtain information from books. Talk about the importance of pictures. Illustrate this by showing the pupils the reading book/'big book', and discussing the information conveyed in the pictures, without reference to the text or title. Explain that illustrations can be just as useful in books intended for adults to use, and show the manual, telling the pupils that some of the information is conveyed in the diagram you have chosen.

In churches, we can often find several examples of pictures giving information. Very often, the information is a story. Hundreds of years ago, stories from the Bible were painted straight onto the walls of some churches. Most of the people could not read then, and the paintings meant that they could learn the stories. Another way of showing the stories from the Bible was in stained-glass windows. Discuss what these look like, and show the decorated glass if possible, explaining that this is really painted glass, but it still shows what the windows look like, and how the light shines through the colours. If you have already visited a church with stained-glass windows, talk about the subjects of any windows you noted. Either:

- remind the pupils of the story of Jonah (page 26), the man through the roof (page 60), or the feeding of the five thousand (page 66), or
- choose one of these stories to tell now.

Say that you want the pupils to design their own stained-glass window based on one of these stories/the story. Discuss with them what they think should be in the window, drawing their attention to its shape. Will they produce one big picture, or two/three panels? Settle on what is going into the picture, encouraging them to think about what is really important in the story. Draw the design, acting as the artist yourself, or ask some pupils to do so. (A rough design could be sketched out, maybe with notes. If you wish, the design could be transferred later onto acetate using pens, or glass paints, with outliners, could be used to produce an imitation window to stick onto a real window.) The activity could be followed up in the classroom, and as a follow-up to the visit, by the pupils individually designing their own windows; you could tell the 'artists' a second story while they are working, or pick up on the paragraph below.

Nowadays, stained-glass windows are still being made. Some of them still tell stories from the Bible. Some of them are made to remind people about people who have lived or worked in the area. Some are made to show facts about the area. So the local industries or scenery might be shown in the stained glass.

PRAYER

Thank you, God, that we can use our talents to tell other people stories. We can use pictures and we can use words. Thank you for the people who have used their talents for making things to decorate churches and other buildings.

34 Communion Table/Altar

You will need

Note

See note on page 70.

- a table
- children's party tableware: paper cups, plates, table covering, etc.
- a coloured or embroidered tablecloth
- flowers and candles
- a loaf or roll of bread
- a jug of red grape juice/blackcurrant drink
- a glass

Introduction

Start off with the table bare. Ask for volunteers to decorate the table for a child's party. As they work, talk about the ways in which we make the table look special for special meals such as a birthday. Comment on the finished table setting, and ask how they could decorate a table for an adult. Ask the pupils to clear the table for you and to sit down. Many churches, but not all, have a table which they decorate for a special meal. Some churches have a table for this meal, but do not decorate it. It isn't a birthday that they are celebrating, but it is a meal that most people in the church will share.

This meal has several different names. It is celebrated in different ways in different churches. But all of these churches are looking back to the same event, and they are holding this special meal to remember that event. The event was a meal. It was the last meal Jesus shared with his disciples before he died. (If you have used the assembly on the Last Supper, refer to it now, and make any necessary omissions in the following information.) Jesus knew he was about to be killed by his enemies. He had something very important to tell his disciples. The meal was already a special one. It was the Feast of the Passover, when the Jewish people thanked God for rescuing them from being slaves in Egypt, many years before. But Jesus had a new meaning to give to the meal, another reason why it would be a special meal for his friends.

He picked up the bread and broke it into pieces for the disciples. He said, 'This bread is like my body. The bread is broken, and my body will suffer and die for you. Eat bread together like this , and remember me.' He picked up the cup of wine and said, 'This wine is like my blood. Soon, I will lose blood as I die. All of you, drink this together to remember me in the future.'

Christians all over the world still celebrate this special meal. They have many names for it, including the Lord's Supper, the Eucharist, Communion and the Mass. But they are all remembering the same meal Jesus shared with his disciples and what he said to them then. They share bread and wine at the meal. It seems strange that Christians should celebrate Jesus talking about his death. But when Christians share this meal now, they are also remembering that Jesus came back to life again. They believe Jesus died because he loved them, and he wanted them to be able to be God's friends. Although they are sad to remember Jesus' death, they are also celebrating his love for them. So many churches decorate the table on which the bread and wine are placed to show how special this meal is to them.

REFLECTION

Show the pupils the flowers, the cloth, and the candles (unlit), explaining these are some of the ways in which the table might be decorated. Ask for volunteers to decorate the table using these. When they have finished, place the 'wine' and the bread in the centre of the table, and ask the pupils to look at the table and think about the bread and wine's meaning for Christians as you read the following:

Christians eat this special meal together. They feel happy and sad during the meal, as they remember what happened to Jesus. They remember that he died, but they also believe that he came back to life. They believe that he is with them every day.

LINK

Easter section, especially 'The Last Supper', page 84

35 A Banner – Jesus and the children

Note

See note on page 70.

You will need

- an enlarged copy of the drawing of the banner on page 117
- examples of any craft using fabrics – fabric painting, embroidery, collage, tapestry, etc.

Introduction

Ask the pupils to list the different materials they saw in the church – stone, wood, glass, etc.. Comment on what objects were made of each material and why. Did they also see things made out of fabric/cloth? If so, talk about the objects made from this, such as altar cloths and kneelers. They may have seen another use of fabric – to make banners. Talk about what banners are. These are used in some churches today as decorations on the walls or hanging over the congregation. But they are more than just decoration. They are used to teach people something as well. They often have a verse from the Bible on them. There might be a picture to illustrate the Bible verse, too.

Show the pupils the picture of the banner. This is a banner from a church in Wollaton in Nottingham. It was made by a team of people who work together to produce many banners. It is not really just black and white, of course! It is made in bright colours. Ask the pupils what they think it is a picture of. Can they guess who the man is in the middle? Can any of them read the verse for you? This verse comes from this Bible story about Jesus.

Jesus had been working hard all day. He had met many people, and had helped them all. He was tired. His disciples saw a group of women coming to see Jesus. They all had their children with them. The disciples knew that the women wanted Jesus to talk to their children. 'But he's too tired!' the disciples decided. They stopped the women, telling them not to bother Jesus. 'He has more important things to do!' they told them.

The women were very disappointed. They began to go home, but Jesus saw them. 'Let the children come to me!' he shouted to them. 'I want to meet them. They are very important.' So the women and their children met Jesus after all.

Usually, banners are just like pictures – flat, two-dimensional (explain and illustrate this). But this one is different, because it has a raised part. The face of Jesus actually stands out from the rest of the banner. It is raised and three-dimensional. It was made of alternate layers of muslin (a thin cloth) and P.V.A. glue, laid over a moulded face shape. Then a local artist painted the face on it. Why do the pupils think the banner-making team decided to make Jesus' face in this way?

REFLECTION

In the banner, Jesus is welcoming many children. They are all very different from each other! Christians believe that God welcomes anyone to be his friend – just as Jesus welcomed all the children who came to him. People do not have to be good or do something special first. They believe that God values and loves everyone, with all of their differences from each other. Ask the pupils to decide which of the children on the banner is most like themselves. We are all special and have special talents.

36 Kneelers – Prayer

You will need

Note

See note on page 70.

- (if possible) a kneeler borrowed from a local church
- an enlarged drawing of the kneeler on page 117
- a large sheet of paper
- felt-tips

Introduction

Ask the pupils to imagine that their mother or father has to stay with relatives for a few weeks. They have promised to telephone Mum or Dad every night to tell them everything that has been going on. Ask the pupils to help you make a list of the sort of things Mum or Dad would want to know, and what sort of thing they would want to tell Mum or Dad (what has happened at school, any problems the pupil has, games they played with their friends, what made them happy, what made them sad, etc.). These are all the sort of things that the pupils share with their families every day. They share many of these with their friends as well. Talking to God is like this for Christians. They believe that God wants them to share their news every day, and that he cares whether they have had a good day or a bad day. They believe that he wants them to tell him when they need his help. They believe that he cares whether they are happy or sad. When Christians talk to God like this, they are praying.

Christians believe that they can pray at any time and in any place. They believe that they can pray alone or with other people. On Sundays, Christians often meet together in church to worship God. They sing hymns and listen to the Bible being read. Often, someone then talks to them about the reading from the Bible, talking about its meaning. Another important part of the worship in church is the time they spend in prayer. Sometimes, they all pray in silence. Sometimes, one person prays and the others listen and pray silently with them. Sometimes, several people take it in turns to pray. Christians believe that talking to God is very important, just as talking to their other friends is important. But prayer isn't just talking. It is also listening. If the pupils talked to their friend, but didn't listen to what their friend had to say, the friendship would not last very long. In a friendship, people listen to each other. Christians often have a time of silence during their prayers, so that they can hear God speaking to them.

There are many different ways of praying. Some Christians pray sitting down, some pray standing up. Some hold their hands palms together, others raise their hands above their heads. Some Christians pray kneeling down. They do this to show how important they believe God is to them. Some churches make kneeling down more comfortable by using kneelers. These are pads to protect their knees from the hard floor. Sometimes, kneelers are decorated with and stitched in bright colours. (Talk about any designs you have seen; Christian symbols such as the fish are often used.)

REFLECTION

Show the pupils the drawing of a kneeler. If they have already heard the story of Daniel, ask them what part prayer played in it. If not, tell it briefly now, from a children's Bible, or from page 24. Draw Daniel praying (kneeling down, arms upraised), and ask the pupils to spend a few moments thinking about how important prayer was to Daniel. Prayer was very important to people in the Bible, and it is very important to Christians today. End by reminding the pupils how important it is to listen as well as to talk to our friends.

Note

Some churches have a low rail for use as a 'kneeler': others have no provision at all. Many denominations do not kneel during public worship, and kneeling is optional in others. Prayer is an important feature of worship in all of them, and this assembly can be used as an introduction to this, whichever denomination is visited.

LINK

'Daniel', page 24; 'Samuel', page 22

37 Telling the Story

You will need

- a diary (if possible, large enough for this book to be held inside it, to look as if you are reading from the diary)
- a Bible

Introduction

Talk about diaries, showing the pupils the spaces for each day's entry in the diary. Ask them to make up and share one-sentence entries for their own diaries. Diaries are a good way of learning about people. In them, we can read what the people themselves said and thought and did. But not everyone keeps a diary. Some people write a book about their lives. In it, they write down things they did, and what they thought and said. This is called an autobiography. This word simply means that the book is written by the person it is about. Sometimes people write books about someone else's life. These are called biographies.

Show the pupils the Bible. This book actually has many shorter books inside it. Four of these are biographies of Jesus. Find Matthew, Mark, Luke and John and show them to the pupils. Most of what we know about Jesus' life is in these four books. These books were written a long time ago, soon after the events which are described in them. They were written to tell other people about Jesus. At first, the people who had known Jesus, especially the disciples, travelled around telling others all about him. As the years passed, many of the people died who had met Jesus and who had known him well. Soon, there would be no one left who had actually met Jesus during his life on earth. If a message is passed on from person to person, it can easily go wrong. People forget bits of the message or get them wrong. Jesus' followers did not want this to happen. They wanted other people to know as much about Jesus as they did, and they wanted to make sure that people heard only what Jesus had really done and said. They knew that some people already were making up stories about Jesus. So his followers realized that they must write down everything they remembered so that other people in the future would know what Jesus had done and what he had taught them about God.

The person who wrote one of these four books was called John. Many people think that he was one of Jesus' disciples. Before Jesus asked him to follow him, John had been a fisherman. He became one of the three most important disciples. We don't know if he kept a diary or not. He was probably too busy! But we can guess what he might have written because we know what he wrote in his biography of Jesus. Show the pupils the first page of John's Gospel. The next set of assemblies is based on diary entries which John might have written about what happened before and after Jesus' death.

The four books that tell about Jesus' life are called Gospels. This word means 'good news'. The books were called this because Christians believe that the news about Jesus and his life and death and resurrection is good news, because it teaches people about God's love.

PRAYER

Thank you, God, that we can learn so much about people who lived a long time ago or who live far away from us. Thank you that we have books and television, computers and other people to tell us what we want to know.

LINK

'The Bible as a Light', page 46, 48

38 Palm Sunday

You will need

- a diary (if possible, large enough for this book to be held inside it, to look as if you are reading from the diary)

Introduction

Remind the pupils of the format of these assemblies: the story of the events before and after Jesus' death are being told as if John had kept a diary. Remind them that we do not know what John would really have written, but these diary entries are based on what he wrote in his Gospel in the Bible.

Have the pupils ever taken part in a welcome for someone famous – perhaps a member of the royal family, a pop star or a football team? If not, perhaps they have seen crowds welcoming people like this on television. Ask them what people do when they welcome famous people. John saw Jesus being welcomed to the city of Jerusalem.

JOHN'S DIARY

We arrived at Jerusalem today. Some of us still feel it is too dangerous to be here. We are sure that Jesus' enemies will try to stop him speaking to the people. But Jesus said that he had to come here. The city is very crowded, of course, because it's the Feast of the Passover. People have come here from miles around, so that they can celebrate the festival in Jerusalem and the Temple. Many of us came here each year when we were children. I know that Jesus used to travel up from Nazareth. Then, we were just part of the crowd. It was very different today. Jesus found a donkey, and he rode into the city on that. We were surprised. After seeing all the wonderful things he has done, we did not expect him to ride into the city on a little donkey! The people were so pleased to see him! In fact, some even came right out of the city to meet him as soon as they heard he was coming! They broke great palm branches off the trees at the side of the road, and waved them high over Jesus. They kept on shouting, 'Hosanna!' and 'Blessed is the King of Israel!' All of this for a carpenter from Nazareth! Like us, they know Jesus is special. But it is hard to understand just how special he is.

REFLECTION

Ask the pupils to think about Jesus' welcome into the city as you read the following:

Riding as a king.
Riding into the city
on a donkey.
Crowds cheering.
Glad to see him.
A few days later,
they wanted him killed.
They watched him die.

Vhen John wrote his Gospel, he said this about Jesus riding into Jerusalem: esus' disciples did not understand what was happening. But afterwards they emembered that a prophet, one of God's messengers, had written hundreds f years before: "See, your king is coming, sitting on a donkey." ' Christians elieve Jesus was that king. When Jesus rode into Jerusalem, some people reeted him as a king. But soon they had all turned against him.

39

The Last Supper

You will need

- a diary (if possible, large enough for this book to be held inside it, to look as if you are reading from the diary)

Introduction

Remind the pupils of the format of these assemblies: the story of the events before and after Jesus' death are being told as if John had kept a diary. Remind them that we do not know what John would really have written, but these diary entries are based on what he wrote in his Gospel in the Bible.

Talk about special meals the pupils have been to. What makes these meals special? Talk about the food, the decorations, etc. Sometimes, when we remember a meal, we realize it was special even though it was an ordinary meal at the time. Perhaps it was special because we met a new friend or just because we had a good time. Jesus shared a meal with his disciples just before he died. It was a special meal anyway, because it was during the Feast of the Passover, which was very important to the Jews. They ate special food and thought about God's love (see Book 1, page 9). But when the disciples looked back at this meal, they realized it was now special for several other reasons, too, even though they did not know this at the time.

JOHN'S DIARY

It has been a terrible evening. I can hardly believe what has happened. Jesus has been arrested! He is on trial now. I fear that his enemies want to kill him. We met together earlier to share the Passover meal with Jesus. We had done this before, of course, but this year it was different right from the start. Jesus was obviously worried about many things. Then he said, 'One of you is going to betray me to my enemies. One of you is going to make it easy for my enemies to arrest me.' We were all horrified, of course. We all wondered who would do this terrible thing to our friend. My friends asked me to ask Jesus to tell us who it was. Jesus said that it would be the one who he gave a piece of bread to. Then he gave Judas a piece of bread, and said, 'Go and do what you have to do quickly.' We just thought he was sending Judas to pay some bill or something, for Judas looks after our money. But now I know that Judas was going to Jesus' enemies, to tell them where Jesus would be later on tonight so that they could arrest him. So Judas left us. Jesus then upset Peter, by saying that Peter would let him down soon. 'You will tell people you do not even know me!' he said. Peter said that he would never behave like this, but Jesus said that he would.

We were all upset by now, and then Jesus started talking about leaving us. He said that soon he would no longer be with us. He told us again how he loved us. He said, 'Soon you will not be able to see me, but after a little while, you will be able to see me again. But then I will leave you again, for I will go back to God, my Father.' We were all so puzzled by this time! Jesus prayed then, asking God to strengthen him and to help us. Then we went out to the Garden of Gethsemane, where Jesus often goes when he wants to talk to God. There, Judas came up to Jesus — and soldiers followed him and arrested Jesus. They dragged him off, and now we are waiting to see what is going to happen to him.

Peter did say he didn't know Jesus, just as Jesus had said he would. Three times, he said he didn't even know Jesus, because he was afraid that he would be arrested too. So John soon knew what Jesus had meant about Peter. But he had to wait a longer time to find out what Jesus had meant about leaving them.

PRAYER

Thank you for your love, Jesus.
Your friends left you.
Your enemies were trying to kill you.
You knew you would die.
But you still carried on.

LINK

'Communion Table/Altar', page 74

40 Jesus' Death

You will need

- a diary (if possible, large enough for this book to be held inside it, to look as if you are reading from the diary)

Introduction

Remind the pupils of the format of these assemblies: the story of the events before and after Jesus' death are being told as if John had kept a diary. Remind them that we do not know what John would really have written, but these diary entries are based on what he wrote in his Gospel in the Bible.

Have the pupils ever had to do something they didn't want to do, but which they knew they had to do? Ask them to think about how they felt for a few moments. John had something to do which he didn't want to do. He had to watch his friend Jesus dying. But he knew that he had to be there, to be with Jesus for as long as he could.

JOHN'S DIARY

Jesus is dead. His enemies got what they wanted and persuaded the Roman Governor to sentence Jesus to death. He was taken out of Jerusalem and fastened to a cross on a hill outside the city. I was frightened, but I wanted to stay with Jesus as long as I could. I stood as near to the cross as the soldiers would let me, and Mary, Jesus' mother, was there with me, and Mary Magdalene and some of Jesus' other friends. Jesus saw us standing there. He asked his mother to look after me as if I were her son, and he asked me to look after her as if she were my mother. So she's here with me now, and she can live with me for the rest of her life. She is very unhappy. We will never forget standing there, watching Jesus die. Just before he died, Jesus suddenly said, 'It's finished!' But he didn't sound as if he was sad. He sounded as if he had managed to finish something that was very difficult. He sounded as if he had won! I don't understand.

Afterwards, two men went to the Roman Governor and asked if they could bury Jesus' body. This was very brave of them. Most of us who were friends with Jesus don't feel safe at the moment. We are hiding away. These two men were secret friends of Jesus. I know that one of them came to visit him at night because he didn't want others to know. But here they were, bravely speaking to the Governor. They took Jesus' body, and poured sweet-smelling spices on it before wrapping it up. They put it in the new tomb one of them had had made ready to use for himself. I've just come back from there. They have rolled a huge stone over the doorway. Some of the women want to go to the tomb after the day of rest. They want to pour their own spices and oils on the body. It is the last thing any of us can do for Jesus now. I still can't believe that he is dead, and that our friendship with him is ended.

It must have seemed to John and to the other disciples that everything had come to an end. They had given up their usual lives to follow Jesus, and they had spent three years with him. They had seen him do many wonderful things, and listened to him as he taught them about God. Now they were alone and frightened in Jerusalem, and they had lost their friend.

PRAYER

Thank you for your love, Jesus.
You were dying, but you thought about your friend and your mother.
You could have saved yourself, but you carried on.

REFLECTION

Christians believe that Jesus could have saved himself from dying. They believe that he carried on because he knew that this was the only way he could help people become friends with God.

LINK

Crosses section, pages 92–99

41 Jesus Is Alive Again!

You will need

- a diary (if possible, large enough for this book to be held inside it, to look as if you are reading from the diary)

Introduction

Remind the pupils of the format of these assemblies: the story of the events before and after Jesus' death are being told as if John had kept a diary. Remind them that we do not know what John would really have written, but these diary entries are based on what he wrote in his Gospel in the Bible.

Play a game of opposites: divide the pupils into two teams, and ask for the opposite (word or phrase) to the words you give them alternately. Ask them to put up their hands, and you will choose who is to answer. If one team doesn't know, the other team can try for a bonus. Some suggested words are:

- hot
- dark
- complete
- open
- inside
- alive
- brave
- happy
- end
- above
- enemy
- up

On the third day after Jesus died, John and the other disciples had a great surprise – one that turned many of their feelings into their opposites! Here is John's story of that day:

JOHN'S DIARY

Something amazing has happened. It seems unbelievable, but all of us have seen him. Jesus is alive again! I wrote that the women wanted to go to the tomb with spices. Well, Mary Magdalene went very early — and found that the stone had been rolled away. At first she thought that someone must have stolen the body. She came running to the house we were staying in, and told us. Peter and I ran to the tomb. It was empty! I looked at the empty tomb. Could it be possible that Jesus was alive? You see, I didn't understand then that Jesus had come back to life, and that some of God's messengers had said this would happen, many years ago. Peter and I went back to the house, leaving Mary near the tomb. She says she saw someone who she thought must be the gardener, and asked him where the body had been taken. The man just said her name — and she realized that this was Jesus, alive once more! She rushed back to us to tell us what had happened.

That night, we were all in the house with the door locked. We still feared that Jesus' enemies would come to arrest us. We were talking about what had happened — when suddenly, Jesus himself was there with us! It was wonderful! He explained everything to us and we understood at last what he had said at the meal we had shared, and why he had died. We understood why Jesus had said, 'It is finished!' as if he had won.

We were all there except for Thomas. He arrived later. When we told him about Jesus, he said he couldn't believe it until he saw Jesus himself. I'm not surprised he said this! It is amazing. I think Jesus will see him soon, so that he can be as happy as we are.

Jesus did see Thomas soon. He came back to the same room when Thomas was with the disciples, just so that Thomas could see him for himself. So Thomas too found out that their friend was alive again.

PRAYER

Thank you, God, for the good news of Easter Day – that Jesus was alive again.

REFLECTION

Jesus being alive once more changed the disciples' lives –
sorrow to joy
despair to hope
feeling alone to having a friend
fear to feeling safe.
Christians believe that Jesus can still change their lives and their feelings like this when they become his friends.

LINK

Crosses section, pages 92–99

42 Picnic on the Beach

You will need

- a diary (if possible, large enough for this book to be held inside it, to look as if you are reading from the diary)

Introduction

Remind the pupils of the format of these assemblies: the story of the events before and after Jesus' death are being told as if John had kept a diary. Remind them that we do not know what John would really have written, but these diary entries are based on what he wrote in his Gospel in the Bible.

Ask two friends to hold hands (both hands, arms crossed) in front of the others. Talk about friendship, and how it is sometimes broken by the things we do or say to each other. (Ask the pupils to let go of hands.) If one friend hurts the other, how can the friendship be mended? Talk about saying sorry, and ask one pupil to hold the other's left hand with their right hand. But this is not enough to mend the friendship completely. The person who was hurt has to forgive the other as well. Ask the other pupil to take their friend's left hand in their right hand, so their arms are joined once more.

Ask the pupils if they can remember what Peter had done to hurt Jesus. We know that Jesus went to Peter soon after he came back to life. Peter probably said sorry straight away. But Peter and the other disciples needed to know that Peter had been forgiven as well. John tells the story of how this happened.

JOHN'S DIARY

I've just got back from a picnic on the beach. But it wasn't just any picnic! Jesus was there. In fact, he cooked the fish for us. Nothing smells better than fish cooking in the early morning on a quiet beach after you've just spent all night fishing! We've been back here in Galilee for several days now. We are still not sure what we should do. Jesus is alive, and we have seen him several times. But we often remind each other that he said he was going back to be with God, his father, soon. We believe he wants us to tell others about him and about God's love for them, but he has told us that we are not to start doing this yet. So some of us decided to go out fishing together. My brother and I and Peter and Andrew were there, just as we had worked together years ago as fishermen. Thomas and some more of Jesus' friends joined us. We collected the fishing nets and climbed into the boat. We four fishermen soon rowed out to the middle of the lake and we threw the nets into the water.

Well, we fished all night — but we caught nothing! Then, just as it was getting light, someone shouted to us from the shore. 'Throw your net over the other side,' he said. Well, we thought we might as well try it. So we did — and the net filled with so many fish that it was too heavy to pull into the boat! I realized who it was, and said to Peter, 'It's Jesus!' Peter immediately leapt into the water and swam for the shore! He wanted to be with Jesus as soon as he could. The rest of us followed, and there was some fish, all ready for us to eat. We enjoyed the meal with Jesus. At the end, he and Peter talked together. We found out that Jesus had again asked Peter to be one of our leaders and to teach other people about God. Peter was much happier after this. He knew Jesus had forgiven him for letting him down so badly when he said he didn't know him.

PRAYER

Help us to remember, God, that we need to say sorry when we have hurt people. Help us to remember too that we need to forgive others when they really are sorry for hurting us.

43 The Cross

You will need

- various badges showing membership or support of organizations, e.g. Beavers/Cubs/Rainbows/Brownies; fan clubs; charity appeals; school badges

Introduction

Talk about badges, displaying those you have selected, and how they can show that the person wearing them belongs to an organization or club, or agrees with whatever is shown on the badge. Break down what the symbols/words on one or two mean, including the school badge if your school has one. Talk about the symbols on them and their use – pictures, etc. that stand for something and give a lot of information, even though they are tiny.

'here is another symbol that is worn sometimes just as a piece of jewellery, but vhich means much more than that to many people all over the world. Talk ıbout how the Guiding, etc. badges are used, with some variations, in many ountries. Another symbol that is used in many countries is the cross. It is a ymbol worn by people who are followers of Jesus. Do any of the pupils know vhy Christians chose the cross? Talk about Jesus dying on the cross. Why do :hristians choose to use a symbol of the death of their leader? Talk about why ıe died – Christians believe that he died because he loved them, and that this vas the only way he could make it possible for God and people to be friends. 'alk about the Christian belief that he came back to life, and is alive now.

'he cross is a symbol which has been used for many hundreds of years. It is used ı many different countries all over the world. So many different kinds of rosses are used. Each one has a different history (explain) and each one means omething different to Christians. But the main meaning of the cross is always he same. It reminds Christians of Jesus' death on the cross and of his love for hem. We are going to look at just a few of the many crosses that are used in lifferent parts of the world.

Thank you that Jesus loved his friends so much that he was willing to die for them. Thank you that the cross on which he died is now a sign to other people of his love and of his friends.

'Jesus' Death', page 86, and 'Jesus Is Alive Again!', page 88

44 St. Brigid's Cross – A symbol of helping others

You will need

- examples or pictures of corn dollies
- (if possible) straw
- dried grass stems
- picture of an even-armed cross (see page 118)

Introduction

Show the pupils the corn dollies. Some of you might have seen some of these. Does anyone know what they are? Talk about corn dollies – what are they made of? Discuss the different shapes that can be created. Even things like swans can be made, just from the dead stalks of wheat or barley like these! People used to make these at Harvest time as part of their celebrations that the grain had been gathered in safely to feed them during the next year. There was once a woman who made something like these but out of a sort of dried grass instead. She made it as a celebration too – but not of the Harvest.

rigid was born in Ireland hundreds of years ago. She heard the story of Jesus vhen she was a young girl, and she decided to become a Christian. She asked esus to be her friend. When she grew up, she decided to become a nun. This neant that she lived with a group of other women and spent most of her time raying and looking after other people. When she became a nun, she chose a erse from the Bible to be her special verse. It said, 'The people who are kind o others and look after them are happy, and God will look after them.' All nrough her life, Brigid tried to do this – to look after other people. She was lways giving away her belongings to other people who needed them. Once, ne gave away her father's sword to an ill person who had no money! She ravelled all over Ireland, helping anyone who needed her help, and looking fter the people in the terrible prisons of the time. Once she and the other uns had prepared a marvellous meal for some important leaders in the nurch. But before they arrived, some people came to the door who had no noney and no food. Brigid took all the food they had got ready – and gave it o the poor people at the door!

ne day, Brigid was looking after a man who was very ill. She prayed for him, nd then, while he was sleeping, she picked up some dried reeds off the floor. n those days, people used to gather a sort of grass called reeds and spread nem on their floors, to keep out draughts and make the floor softer to walk n. Brigid chose some stems from the reeds, and plaited them into the shape f the cross. (Show the pupils the picture of the even-armed cross.) The man voke up and asked her what she was making. She showed him the cross and old him about Jesus, who had died on a cross because he loved his friends. The nan listened carefully, and then said, 'I would like to be one of Jesus' friends, oo.'

ll through her life, Brigid worked hard to help others and to tell others about esus and his love. This cross (show the picture again) is now called Brigid's ross and reminds people of her life.

PRAYER

Thank you, God, for the people who have worked to tell others about you and about your love for them.

REFLECTION

Ask the pupils to look at the picture of St. Brigid's Cross once more. It is many hundreds of years since St. Brigid made a cross like this. The cross means the same to Christians now as it did to her so long ago. It still tells them about Jesus' love.

45 The Sudanese Cross – A symbol of hope

You will need

- pairs of smooth bamboo canes (ends blunted and taped over if necessary) 18 cm (7 inches) and 8 cm (3 inches) long, painted black (or covered with black tape), and made into crosses (see page 118) before the assembly using sticky tape or thread
- an enlarged copy of the cross on page 118
- yellow insulating tape
- an atlas or world map
- an adult helper briefed on how to make the cross

Introduction

Talk about hope, discussing what it means. Make up a sentence about something you hope for – e.g. 'I hope it will be nice weather today.' Ask the pupils for sentences saying what they hope for. Explain that people in some countries hope for peace more than anything else. The Dinka people of Southern Sudan (show them where this is) have been in the middle of a civil war for many years (explain what this is). Many have been killed, and others have gone to other countries as refugees (explain this). Some have been captured, and many have been unable to earn money or grow crops to feed their families. All through this trouble, more and more of the Dinka people have become Christians. They have made a special cross, one which they could not have made without the war. Ask for pairs of volunteers to copy you as you make one.

Core material

The Dinkas' cross is made from a very hard, black wood called ebony (indicate the canes which represent this). The Dinkas cut two pieces of ebony, and fasten them together to make the cross (show them the crosses and the picture of the cross). Then they decorate it. (As you talk, wrap the insulating tape around the cross to represent the bronze. A second adult might be needed to help the pupils

decorate their crosses.) They use bronze, a metal alloy, made from copper and tin. This has been beaten flat, and it is then wrapped round the wood. The Dinka people do not make the bronze: they find it! The bronze is from the cases of the cartridges (like bullets) which were used and fired in the civil war. There was a lot of fighting in their country, and many thousands of shots were fired. It is easy for them to find enough cartridge cases to decorate the crosses. When they hold special celebrations, they carry these crosses high above their heads. They are a symbol of peace, made from the rubbish war has left behind.

Christians believe that Jesus can bring them peace even in the middle of war and sorrow. They mean they can still feel that he is with them and that he loves them, no matter what is happening. They believe that, when they are unhappy, Jesus is unhappy too. He understands how they feel and he suffers with them. Because they believe he is with them, they can feel peaceful even when things are going wrong. They believe that he is still looking after them and that he knows everything that is happening. So the cross reminds them of their belief that Jesus is with them every day, helping them and loving them.

Christians also believe Jesus will bring a different kind of peace one day. They believe that one day, there will be no more wars or hunger or sorrow, because Jesus will be king of all the earth. There is a verse in the Bible which talks about this time. It says: 'The people will make their swords into ploughs and their spears into pruning knives. No country will fight another country, and no one will train to be soldiers any more.' (Isaiah 2.4) Explain that ploughs and pruning knives are used in farming, but that farming can only take place when a country is at peace. The people of Sudan could not grow their crops when people were fighting on their land. So this verse talks about a time when no one will need weapons to fight other people. Instead, all the people will be able to live in peace at home, and grow the food they need. The people of Sudan might think about this verse when they look at their special cross. The cross is a symbol of hope to them, reminding them of their belief that Jesus will bring peace one day even to their country which has suffered so much.

PRAYER

Ask the pupils to hold up their crosses so that the others can see them as you pray.
Thank you, God, that the cross is a symbol of peace, even in the middle of trouble and fighting. Thank you for your promise to bring peace to your friends.

REFLECTION

Ask the pupils to think about a time when they feel peaceful. Do they think it is possible to feel peaceful if other people are angry with us, or if we are angry with other people? Ask them to think about how they can help themselves and other people to feel peaceful.

46 The Mexican Star Cross – A symbol of joy

You will need

- an atlas or world map
- lengths of brightly coloured wool
- lollipop sticks or plastic straws joined in pairs with wool in even-armed cross shape
- a completed Mexican Star Cross (see page 117)
- streamers, balloons, etc. (see below)
- adult helpers briefed on how to make the cross

Introduction

Talk about celebrations and the objects we use to show we are celebrating – such as streamers, balloons, etc. – and ask the pupils to demonstrate with any you have. Use party poppers yourself. Have any of the pupils seen street parades or festivals, such as carnival? Talk about the use of costumes and floats. In many countries, there are street celebrations and parades to celebrate religious festivals, such as Easter. Remind the pupils why Christians celebrate Easter, even though Jesus died on Good Friday (see pages 86 and 88). In one country, a special sort of cross is used in the Easter celebrations.

Show the pupils where Mexico is. In this country and in other South American countries, there are colourful and lively parades at Easter. The floats and the churches are decorated with bright colours, to show the people's joy that it is Easter, the time when Jesus came back to life. Many Mexican Christians make a cross to use as a decoration in these celebrations. It is called a Mexican Star Cross – show them the completed cross. Invite pupils to make their own crosses: adult help is needed until the pupils have caught the pattern of making the cross. Invite them to choose their own colour scheme for their cross, and set them to work. (They will not finish this in the assembly: make sure they understand you are not expecting them to finish it now. Perhaps they could be given adequate wool to complete the cross at home, and be invited to show the finished product as part of a later assembly. Alternatively, the pupils and their helpers can be put to work at the very beginning of the assembly.)

These crosses are very bright and colourful. Many different designs can be made. Their brightness reflects the joy felt by the Mexican Christians as they celebrate Easter. Christians all over the world celebrate this joy. Many churches in this country will use special colours and flowers to decorate their churches. Candles will be lit, and people will greet each other with the words 'Christ is risen!' and the reply 'He is risen indeed!'

Mexican Christians are just some of many thousands of Christians celebrating the same event all over the world. Christians believe that they are like one big family, all celebrating the same joy, because they believe Jesus is alive and is with them as their friend.

PRAYER

Thank you, God, for the joy that Christians all over the world feel as they think about Jesus at Easter.

47 We Are Marching in the Light of God

Note

This assembly can be used after the assemblies on pages 44 and 46.

Introduction

Recap on what has been said in the assemblies about bringing light to other people and about living in the light of the Bible. This song brings these ideas together. It is sung by Christians in South Africa and has become very popular with Christians in this and other countries too. It contains the idea of living as God wants his friends to live – and obeying what he says in the Bible. It is also a song of hope. Because Christians are God's friends, they live in his light.

Read the words to the pupils. The song can be taught without the words in italics; these could be clapped in rhythm or just played on the piano. But most pupils will be able to learn to use this tune as well. Invite the pupils to think of a suitable movement to accompany the song. It is not easy to stand still while singing it. A suitable accompaniment could be worked out on simple percussion instruments.

REFLECTION

Play the music quietly while the pupils think about the way light helps us.

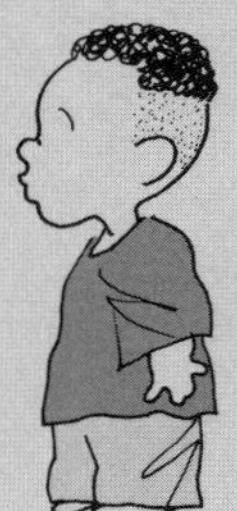

LINK

Light section; assembly about South Africa, page 40

Song for **'We Are Marching in the Light of God'** *(page 100)*

We Are Marching in the Light of God

Words: African origin, collected and edited by Anders Nyberg
Music: African melody, scored by Notman KB, Ljungsbro
and Lars Parkman, arranged by R.T. Walker

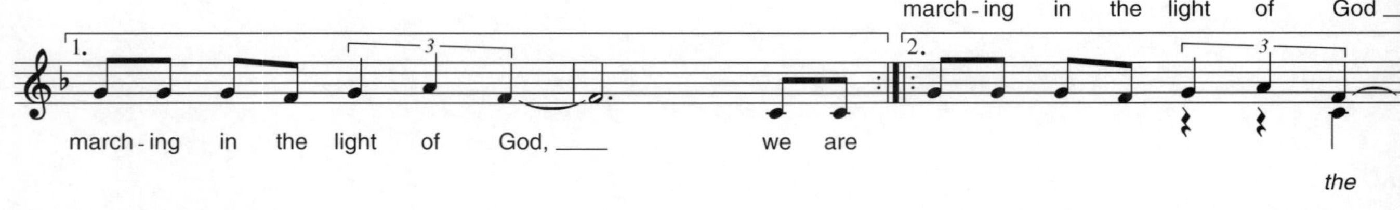

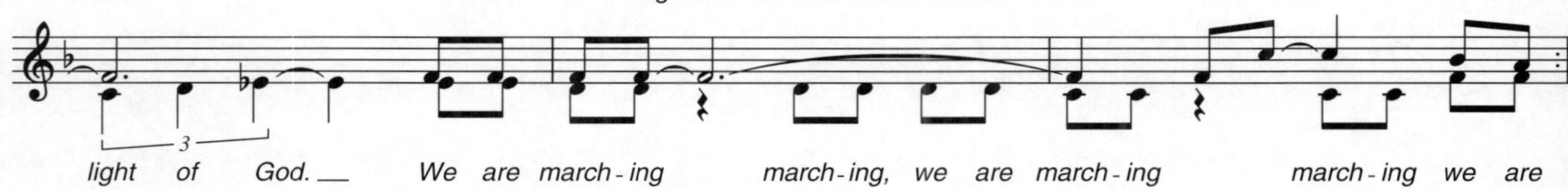

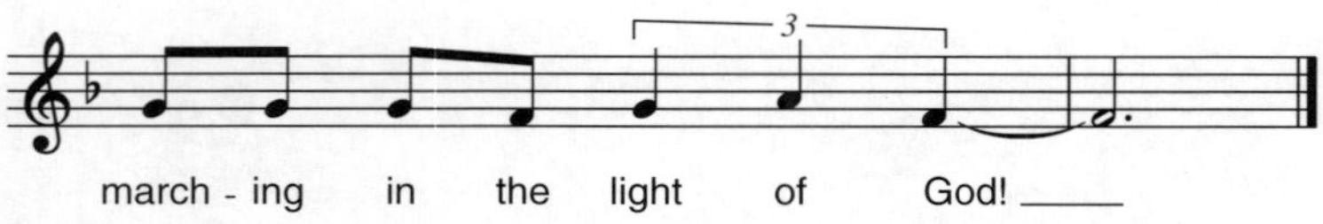

Words: African origin collected and edited by Anders Nyberg. *Music:* African melody scored by Notman KB, Ljungsbro and Lars Parkman. Arranged by R.T. Walker. Used with the kind permission of Iona Community/Wild Goose Publications, Glasgow, Scotland.

We Are Marching in the Light of God

Song for **'The Feeding of the Five Thousand'** *(page 104)*

The Feeding of the Five Thousand

48 The Feeding of the Five Thousand

Note

This assembly follows on from the assembly on the feeding of the five thousand, page 66.

You will need

- (if appropriate to the age and ability of the pupils) a copy of the words (see page 103)

Introduction

Ask the pupils to retell the story of The Boy's Packed Lunch. This song also tells the story of this giant picnic. The chorus is sung by the crowd themselves. Ask the pupils what the crowd would have been thinking at the beginning of the story and at the end. Then read the words of the two choruses, and discuss how well the pupils' ideas matched the words of the chorus.

Teach the words and music of the chorus, preferably by the 'listen and copy' technique, in which the leader sings a line, and the pupils copy it. When the pupils are confident of the words and tune, ask them how the crowd would have sung each chorus – how they would have felt and sounded in each. Ask the pupils to sing the choruses again, trying to convey these feelings to their 'audience'. Discuss how the first chorus (the first singing of 'We are hungry') sets the scene, making the hearers wonder what is going to happen. If time allows, the pupils can learn the verses as well. If not, the leader can sing these, with the pupils just joining in for the choruses.

Note

If appropriate, the assembly 'The Boy's Packed Lunch' can be presented to parents with the song incorporated at the relevant points in the story.

REFLECTION

Jesus knew what the crowd needed at that giant picnic. Christians believe that Jesus still knows what they need. They believe that he will give them everything they need. But this might not be the same as what they think they need!

LINK

'The Boy's Packed Lunch', page 66

49 Light

Note

This assembly can follow the series of assemblies on Light. It picks up the themes of sources of light and of Jesus as the Light of the World.

You will need

- a copy of the words on page 108 (if appropriate to the age and ability of the pupils)

Introduction

Recap on the work the pupils did on sources of light, and ask them which of these sources were natural and not man-made. This song talks about these natural sources of light. Read the words of the three verses, explaining any words with which they are not familiar. Then read the words of the chorus, and recap on what was said about Jesus as the Light of the World.

ivide the pupils into two groups, and teach one group the verse. Teach the ther group the chorus. If possible, use the 'listen and copy' technique, line by ne. The pupils can then sing the song as two groups 'answering' each other. ncourage the group singing the verses to think about the different qualities f the light mentioned in each verse. Encourage them to think about how they ould reflect this in their singing, taking account of the tone used, use of accato or legato, and the volume for each verse. They can then sing the three erses, and the other group can comment upon whether they have achieved a ontrast between them or not.

ome pupils might like to make up simple actions to go with the words. If so, end time talking about the different qualities of the light from sun, moon nd stars.

REFLECTION

The Reflection on page 47 can be used again here.

LINK

Light section

Song for **'Light'** *(page 106)*

Light

Song for **'Jonah'** *(page 110)*

(**NB** The lines in the brackets are intended to be sung as an echo.)

50 Jonah

Note

This assembly is to be used after the assembly on Jonah, page 26.

Introduction

Talk about echoes and what they are. Say some simple sentences, and then ask for volunteers to repeat them. Then sing a short musical phrase without words, and ask them to echo this. This song tells the story of Jonah, but the pupils can take part without learning a lot of words because they are going to echo you!

Retell the story of Jonah with the pupils' help, concentrating on why Jonah behaved as he did. Explain that they will need to echo parts of the song as you sing it. Agree some signal with them to show which lines they need to echo; for instance, you could raise your hand during the relevant words. Perhaps they can think of something more imaginative! Read through all the words so that they are familiar with them, and then teach them the parts they are to echo.

REFLECTION

The Reflection on page 27 can be used again here.

Music Suggestions

These are suggestions of songs for each section in the book. If they are not suitable for a school, others can be used.

BOOKS USED AND ABBREVIATIONS

JP1 *Junior Praise 1* comp. P. Horrobin & G. Leavers, Marshall Pickering, 1986

ChPr *Children's Praise* comp. G. Leavers & P. Burt, Marshall Pickering, 1991

C&P *The Complete Come and Praise* comp. G. Marshall-Taylor, BBC, 1994

BBP *Big Blue Planet* ed. J. Jarvis, Stainer & Bell and Methodist Church Division of Education and Youth, 1995

FG *Feeling Good* P. Churchill with S. Churchill & J. Godfrey, National Society/Church House Publishing, 1994

R1 *Rejoice One* comp. A.White with A. Byrne & C. Malone, HarperCollins Religious, 1993

C&P Beg *Come and Praise Beginning* comp. G. Marshall-Taylor, B.B.C., 1996

Cel *A Year of Celebration* ed. J. Porter & J. McCrimmon, McCrimmons 1995

SSL *Someone's Singing, Lord* chosen by B. Harrop, A. & C. Black, 1992

SEE *Songs for Every Easter* M. & H. Johnson, Out of the Ark Music, 1995

THIS TIME OF YEAR

We thank you, God, for Mummies; God, you hold me; How beautiful **BBP**

Imagine **Cel**

Don't forget! **SEE**

People we love **FG**

People who help; Lighting the way; We can give; For all that you do; Patching up a quarrel **R1**

Thank you for all the love **ChPr**

Candle time; I'm sorry **FG**

BIBLE CHARACTERS

Sometimes problems can be big; One day I might; I will trust; The best book **ChPr**

Daniel was a man of prayer; Come listen to my tale; When I'm feeling down and sad **JP**

CHOCOLATE BANANAS

1 and 2 and 3 and 4 **C&P Beg**

The chocolate song **SEE**

Always remember, never forget; I like eating **BBP**

(See also ***Other Children*** section suggestions, below.)

OTHER CHILDREN

God has given us eyes to see; If you're black or if you're white; Keep a light in your eyes; Caring, sharing **BBP**

When I needed a neighbour **C&P**

He's got the whole wide world **ChPr**

LIGHT

Jesus bids us shine; This little light of mine; The best book to read **ChPr**

There's a light **C&Pr Beg**

Shine, Jesus, Shine; Imagine **Cel**

Candle time **FG**

Lighting the way **R1**

SENSES: SIGHT

I spy with my little eye; God made the colours **ChPr**

All around **C&P Beg**

Who made your eyes; How beautiful; God has given us eyes to see **BBP**

He gave me eyes; Think of a world **Cel**

Wonderful senses **R1**

JESUS' MIRACLES

Fish and bread; Calming the storm **FG**

Rocking, rocking; It was Jesus; Not 1, not 2, not 3, but 4 **ChPr**

A boy gave to Jesus; Who took fish and bread **JP**

When no one else; Five little loaves **ChPr**

Four friends carry a neighbour; One day when we were fishing **BBP**

CHURCH VISIT ASSEMBLIES

God made furry things; For micro chips, for oven chips **BBP**

God hears me; God created all the earth; Anytime, anywhere; I can talk to God **ChPr**

Picture books **R1**

EASTER

What Jesus did; Lost and found; Great news!; Patching up a quarrel **R1**

Jesus lives again **FG**

We have a king who rides a donkey **SSL**

Trotting, trotting; Jesus in the garden **C&P**

The donkey trotted **C&P Beg**

Jesus called to Peter the fisherman; It's hard to say 'I'm sorry'; Easter tells us **BBP**

Alleluia, alleluia; Praise King Jesus **ChPr**

Celebrate! **SEE**

Easter Alleluia **Cel**

CROSSES

Jesus' love is very wonderful **C&P Beg**

Easter tells us; He came down **BBP**

(See also ***Easter*** section suggestions.)

Banana and sections for **'Fair-share Bananas'** *(page 32)*

7p 3p 2p 3p 3p 2p

Matchbox nets for **'School and Work'** *(page 34)*

GLUE TO BACK OF 'X'

55mm

x

16mm 35mm 16mm 35mm 16mm

14mm 34mm 14mm

55mm

Cut

Cut

Score and Fold

Score and Fold

GLUE TO BACK OF X

180mm

X

40mm 100mm 40mm 100mm 40mm

180mm

38mm 96mm 38mm

Note

Solid outline gives dimensions for a standard matchbox.
Broken outline gives dimensions for a large matchbox suitable for infants.

How to dip candles – for **'Dipping and Making Candles'** *(page 38)*

You will need:

- wax – available by the kilo in many craft shops
- stearin (to be added to the wax in ratio of 2 tablespoons to a kilo of wax)
- an *old* saucepan
- at least two wax dyes (old wax crayons can be used, but do not always give such a clear colour)
- two empty, washed baked bean cans to hold the wax – take care with sharp edges
- a large bucket of cold water, readily accessible

Fill the cans with the wax and stearin mixture, and stand them in water in the saucepan (the cans will mark the base, so it's important to use an old one). Heat the water until it is very hot and the wax begins to melt, then turn down the heat. Do not let the water boil, or else it may splash into the wax. When the wax is melted, add shavings of the dyes – a little goes a long way! If the wax is melted immediately before the assembly, the wax will stay hot enough to dip the candles.

Remove the cans from the pan, and place on a heatproof surface in view of the pupils, but well away from them. Hold each candle by one end, dip it slowly into the wax, and then into the cold water. The candle can then be held by the other end and dipped into the other colour wax. Various effects can be achieved, even with just two colours.

If any wax splashes onto your hands, put them into the cold water immediately. Put the cans in a safe place, and allow the wax to cool and set completely before attempting to transport it.

Drawing of elephant carving for **'Stone Carvings – An elephant with the wrong ears!"** *(page 70)*

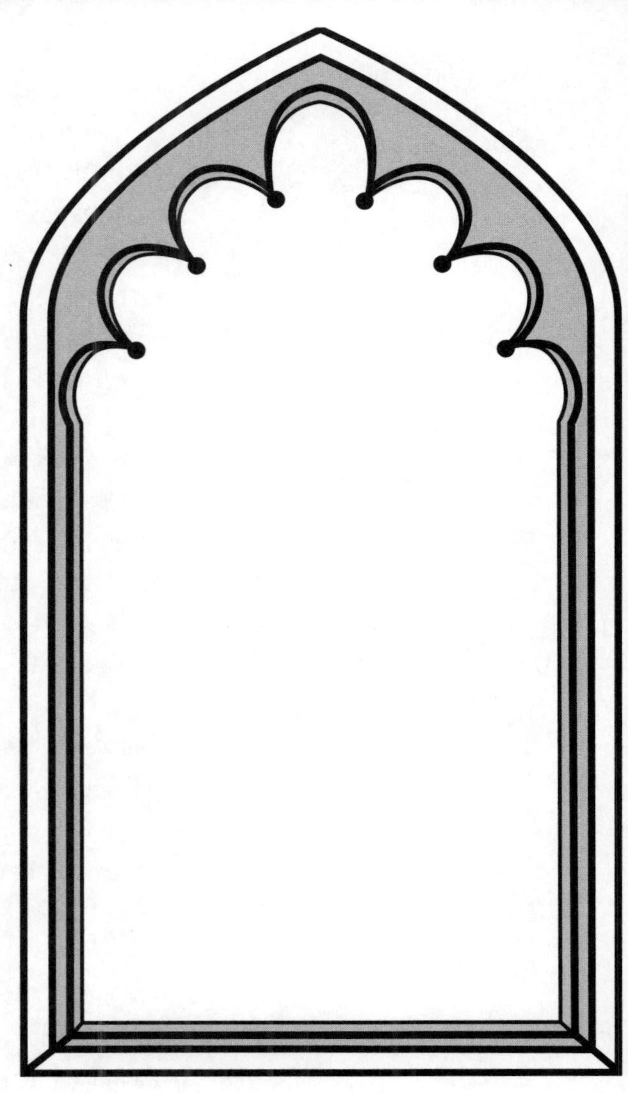

Template for **'Stained-glass Windows'** (page 72)

Drawing for **'A Banner'** *(page 76)*

Drawing for **'Kneelers'** *(page 78)*

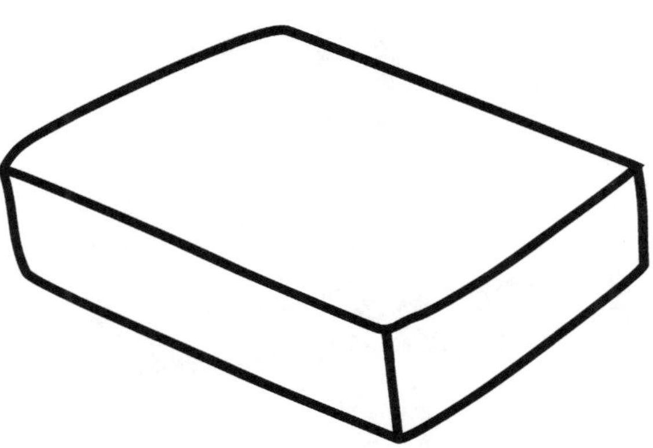

Instructions for **'The Mexican Star Cross'** *(page 98)*

Fasten two lollipop sticks or straws together in an even-armed cross shape. Select one colour of wool, and wind it around the shape, going over and under the arms alternately as you work around the cross, rotating the cross in your hands as you work. Change colour by simply knotting a new colour onto the old one.

Cross for **'The Sudanese Cross'** *(page 96)*

Even-armed cross for **'St. Brigid's Cross'** *(page 94)*

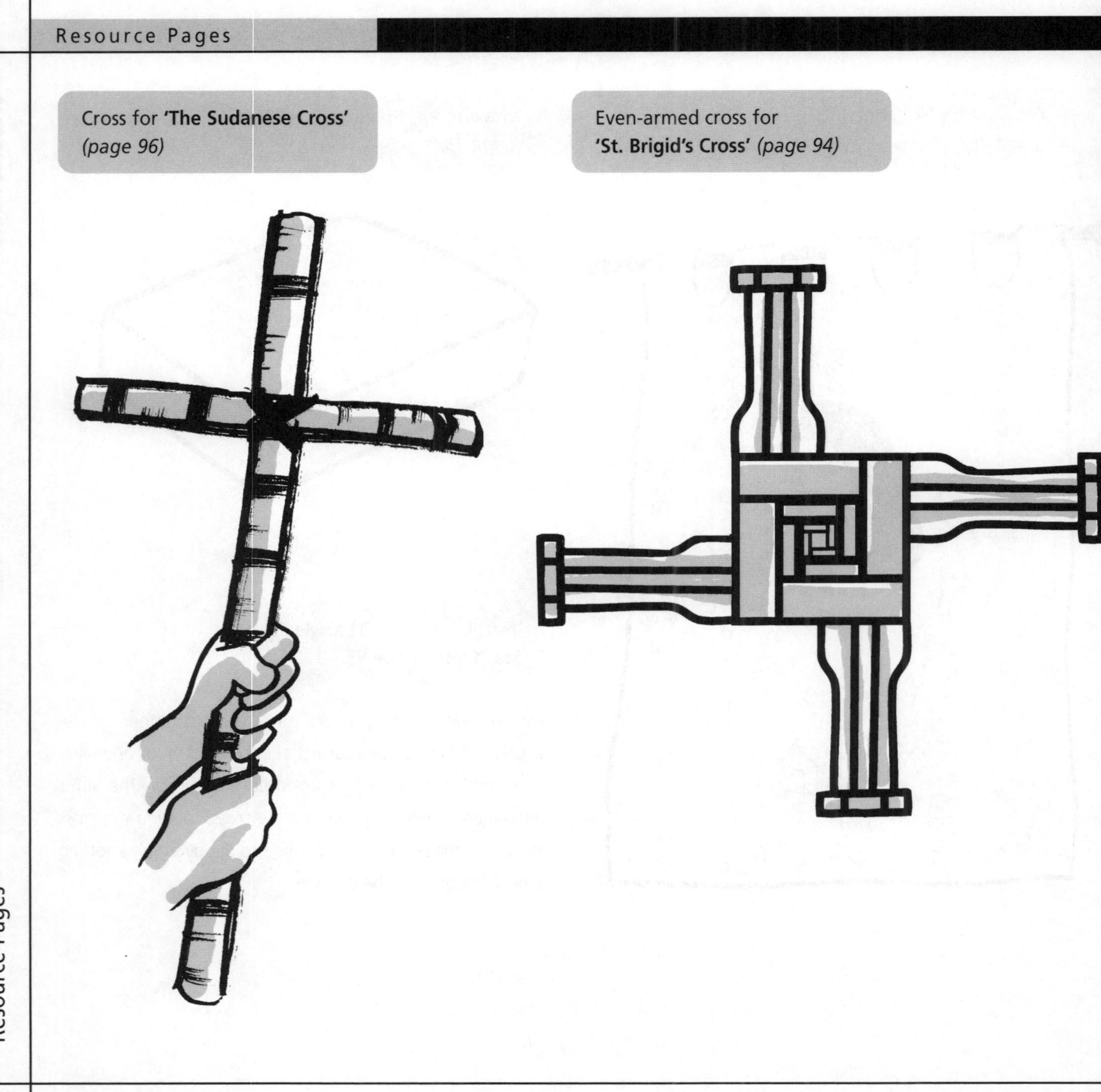

People, Places, Times and Things Index

Thematic Index

Indexes